ALTOONA ACTION

PHOTOGRAPHY BY THOMAS A. BIERY

WRITTEN BY JAIME F. M. SERENSITS

The Railroad Press

PO Box 444
Hanover, PA 17331-0444

The Railroad Press
Publishers of:

TRP Magazine

*Chessie System
Cumberland Action*

ALCO Reference #1

ALCO's to Allentown

CF7 Locomotives

*New England 1930's
Steam Action:
Worcester*

B&M Passenger Cars

*Children's Railroad
Learning & Activity
Book*

Printed in the United States of America.

International Standard Book Number 0-9657709-7-4

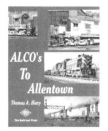

Page 1: A crewmember checks out the inside of his lead EMD on the mainline at Works. Second in command of this train, Penn Central #3086 is a GP40. As usual, there is a lot of activity at Works on this spring day in 1971 -- two helper sets are idling in the distance and the eastbound train on the adjacent track has a GE sandwiched by two EMD's. It looks like there are two RPO's in the storage yard and the jade green cars are starting to outnumber the PRR keystones. Notice also the strange orange load on the flatcar and the panel track in the gons.

Welcome to "Altoona Action". We will begin our journey on the next page at Petersburg, Pennsylvania. This is the location where trains trains could be rerouted over the Hollidaysburg & Petersburg Secondary and up around Muleshoe Curve on the New Portage Secondary as an alternative to the standard mainline routing through Altoona and around Horseshoe Curve. We will head west and make stops at Spruce Creek and Tyrone before covering one of the most famous railroad cities in the world.

The early portions of the book will consist mainly of photographs, as they tell the story best. As you get acquainted with the area, we will advance into slightly more detailed peeks at a truly incredible stretch of mountain railroad.

We have included photos of operations on the Pennsylvania Railroad, Penn Central and Conrail so you can see, in one volume, how this region changed over the years. Not only did the paint and the motive power change, but philosophies changed, as well. Towers fell, tunnels were abandoned and tracks were removed. Some areas saw improvement as a result, while others suffered.

In finding benchmarks to base our timetable information, we have chosen the 1st editions of the Penn Central and Conrail timetables, as these came the closest to reflecting the PRR and PC in their final form. They were too new for wholesale changes to have been made. We hope you enjoy this tribute to Altoona in an era of great change.

ABOVE: In the Summer of 1967, Pennsylvania Railroad SD40 #6086 and GP9B #3823 are at the southern terminus of the Bald Eagle Branch a mile west of Tyrone at Gray Tower (milepost 223.1). They are switching the yard that marks the interchange with this branch and the PRR mainline. You can see Gray Tower behind the GP9B and a crewmember riding a boxcar on the far left side of the photo.

Interlocking	Interlocking Station	Block Station and Train Order Office	Block-Limit Station	HOLLIDAYSBURG & PETERSBURG BRANCH-A H. & P. SECONDARY TRACK-A NEW PORTAGE SECONDARY TRACK-A STATIONS	Distance from Petersburg	Sidings Assigned Direction. Car Capacity 50 ft. cars		
						West or North	East or South	Both
				ALLEGHENY DIVISION PETERSBURG (Main Line)				
X		X		PETE (Main Line)......R-Hunt	0.5			103
				ALEXANDRIA	5.0			
				ALFARATA	6.2			45
				CLOVER CREEK JCT.	16.1			
			X	SPRING......K-Wye (e)	16.1			
				WILLIAMSBURG	18.3			
				GANISTER	20.3			
				FRANKSTOWN	29.5			
			X	FRANK......K-Wye (e)	29.5			
				JONES ST. HOLLBG.	31.5			
				JCT. MOR. COVE TRK.	32.0			
			X	HOLLY......K-Wye (e)	32.2			
				HOLLIDAYSBURG	32.3			
X	P	P ★		WYE	33.4			
X	P	P ★		WYE	33.4			
				ELDORADO	36.6			
X				ELDO.......R-Wye	36.6			
X	X	X ★		ALTO	39.6			
				ALTOONA	39.9			
X	X	P ★		WYE	33.4			
				DU	37.1			
				MS	40.6			
				AH	44.7			
				PS	46.9			
X		X		SF.......R-AR (M. L.)	48.7			180

NOTE—The direction from Petersburg to Altoona is westward.
NOTE (e)—Controlled by Alto when Wye is not in service.

Interlocking, Block and Block-Limit Stations in service part-time as follows:

Station	Hours in Service
WYE	7.00 A.M. Monday to 3.00 P.M. Sunday, except closed Holidays 7.00 A.M. until 7.00 A.M. of the following day.

ABOVE: Bare rock cliffs provide an imposing backdrop for PRR SD40 #6086 and Penn Central GP35 #2396 motoring westbound with a merchandise train near Petersburg, east of the connection to Hollidaysburg and Tunnelhill. Notice the New York Central-style numbers on the battery box of #2396 and the classic Penn Central, Chesapeake & Ohio, PRR and Wabash boxes on the head end.

OPPOSITE ABOVE: West of Spruce Creek on April 17, 1985, Conrail SD40 #6281 is at the helm, but the star of the show is the ailing B23-7. The thick smoke pouring from its stack is obscuring the tonnage of this westbound freight which consists mainly of hi-cube auto parts boxcars. From this elevated vantage point, it's not difficult to see where the recently-removed third track had been.

OPPOSITE BELOW: A spring snow covers the ground in April 1970 as Penn Central GP40 #3112, GP30 #2247, and a NYC GP40 roll a fast eastbound freight through the snow-capped rock cut and under the 2163 signal bridge at Union Furnace. Note the bright red Great Northern boxcar near the front of the train. The "G" plates on the signal bridge allow a westbound tonnage freight to run a red signal at restricted speed. The train is flying down the center of the three track mainline and has just passed the quarry on the other side of the cut.

It's May 1969 and guess what has eased around Horseshoe Curve and down the hill this morning?? How about four E-units on the point of a Flexi-Van train!!! The high-speed gearing of the E-units made them very well suited to hauling fast intermodal freight. The train is well east of Altoona and is about to pass Spruce Tower. These three views show the train bolting down the straightaway past Espy Farms and swinging around the big left-hand curve past the tower. You can see one of the Espy Farms cows getting a drink from the Little Juniata River. In addition to all of the containers, notice the Railway Express boxcar near the front of the train. The road on the hillside is Pennsylvania State Route 45.

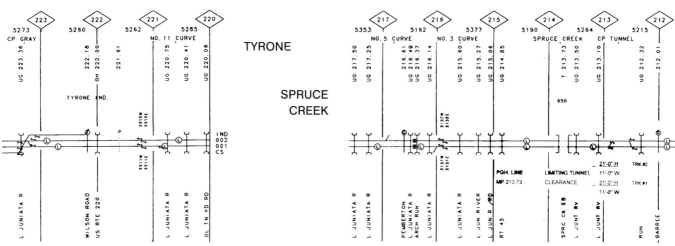

OPPOSITE: Shades of the New York Central! A GP40 acquired new by Penn Central and a former NYC GP40 streak across the Little Juniata River between Spruce Creek and Union Furnace in May 1970 with an eastbound COFC train. The stone arch bridges built by the Pennsylvania Railroad blend in beautifully with the scenery all across its namesake state.

BELOW: Penn Central GP35 #2250 (ex-PRR 2309) and a GE lead a westbound mixed freight into Tyrone in August 1975. With meager power on the head end, this train will certainly need a set of helpers to get over the mountain. Notice that there used to be FIVE tracks here, with the rickety weed-covered track on the left allowing trains coming down from the area around Pennsylvania Furnace to enter Tyrone and connect with the Bald Eagle Branch without fouling the mainline. On Route 453 southeast of Tyrone you can see the remains of the spectacular trestle that was once used by trains heading to and from Pennsylvania Furnace.

Interlocking	Interlocking Station	Block Station and Train Order Office	Block-Limit Station	STATIONS	Distance from Tyrone	West or North	East or South	Both
				BALD EAGLE BRANCH				
X	X	X★		LOCK HAVEN (Nor. Div.)	54.2			
X				POST ....R-Lock Haven	52.5			164
				DIV. POST (Nor. Div.)	52.0			
				ALLEGHENY DIVISION				
X				EAST BEECH......)	47.2			
				BEECH CREEK...	45.9			211
X				WEST BEECH...	45.1			
				HOWARD...	39.7			
X				SAND..	35.9			
X	X	X★		MILES...	30.8			
				MILESBURG...	30.8			123
X				BAKER...	29.4			
				UNIONVILLE.	25.9			
X				EAST JULIAN R-Miles	21.5			
				JULIAN...	21.4			129
X				WEST JULIAN...	20.1			
				MARTHA...	17.2			
X				PORT MATILDA...	13.8			116
X				BEAVER...	9.7			
				EAGLE...	6.1			
				BALD EAGLE...	5.0			
X				VAIL...	3.0			
				PARK	1.5			144
X				17th STREET, TYRONE...	0.9			
				TYRONE.				
X				WILSON ....R-Gray				

The direction from Lock Haven to Wilson is westward.

OPPOSITE: You could see the entire Spruce Creek interlocking plant from the shoulder of PA Route 45. The sun is starting to burn through some of the valley fog as a handful of EMD's skirt the tower with a westbound piggyback train. There are no more signal bridges here and the tower is long gone, disappearing in the 1980's. Despite the roar of the four SD's dragging the train up the stiff grade, the hungry horse in the distance does not even bother looking up as it grazes on the low land along the swollen Little Juniata River.

BELOW: The Scotchlite Express hustles eastbound through the S-curve at Tyrone behind Conrail and Union Pacific power. A Vivitar 285 flash lights up this doublestack as it is about to cross Wilson Road on the last evening of Conrail's existence, Friday, August 21, 1998. The next day would be the first day that Conrail would be controlled by Norfolk Southern and CSX. Operations would not be split by the two railroads until June 1, 1999. The covered hopper cars on the right are on the Conrail / Nittany & Bald Eagle interchange track. The NBER runs from Tyrone to Lock Haven on the former Pennsylvania Railroad Bald Eagle Branch. Photo by Jaime F. M. Serensits.

				BALD EAGLE BRANCH (Allegheny Division)			
Interlocking	Interlocking Station	Block Station and Train Order Office	Block-Limit Station	STATION	Distance From Tyrone	Siding Direction: E.W.N.S. or Both & Length in Feet	Note
X				LOCK HAVEN..........R - Lyco (Main Line Harrisburg to Buffalo)	54.2		
X				POST....................R - Lyco	52.5	8629 B	
X				EAST BEECH..........	47.1		
				BEECH CREEK.......	46.0	9906 B	
X				WEST BEECH..........	45.1		
				HOWARD...............	39.7		
X				MILES...................	30.9		
				(Bellefonte Sec.Trk.)			
				MILESBURG...........	30.9	5997 B	
X				BAKER..................	29.4		
				UNIONVILLE..........	25.9		
X				EAST JULIAN.......... R - Gray	21.5		
				JULIAN..................	21.5	6624 B	
X				WEST JULIAN........	20.3		
				MARTHA...............	17.3		
				PORT MATILDA....	13.8		
				BALD EAGLE..........	5.0		
X				VAIL.....................	3.0		
X				PARK....................	1.5	7200 B	
				17TH ST. TYRONE	0.9		
				TYRONE...............	0.0		
X				WILSON................ (Main Line Phila. to Pittsburgh)			
				The direction from Lock Haven to Wilson is Westward.			

OPPOSITE ABOVE: Penn Central SD40 #6064 and SD45 #6206 power this hot eastbound symbol freight through the reverse curves at Tyrone in late summer 1975. The current Amtrak station is behind the photographer. Around the curve to the west is Gray Tower, where the Bald Eagle Branch to Lock Haven joins the mainline. Today the branch is operated by the Nittany and Bald Eagle Railroad and R.J. Corman utilizes part of the yard for their railway equipment sales. The "fifth" track shown on page 9 is the same one in the foreground of this photo, governed by the smart-looking dwarf signal.

OPPOSITE BELOW: Penn Central E8 #4291 in Tuscan and basic black E8 #4308 are rolling to a stop with "The Duquesne" at Tyrone. Notice that this eastbound consist is headed by Railway Express reefer #7450. The spartan scheme worn by 4291 was an attempt by PRR management to save money when times got tough; the gentleman sauntering across the right of way and the couple waiting on the platform are a typical representation of the sparse patronage afflicting many of the trains of this era. You can once again see the "fifth" track in the background; it makes a wye, affording trains entering the branch from either direction the luxury of not having to turn their power. This photo was taken from the old footbridge at Tyrone. Today you will find a much bigger bridge just around the corner -- the one that carries Interstate 99 over the Norfolk Southern mainline! As this book is being written, Tyrone's brand new "Bud Shuster Intermodal Transportation Center and Rail Park" is being constructed, scheduled to replace the Amtrak "bus shelter" in September 2000.

ABOVE: Two F's and an early Geep trundle into the far reaches of East Altoona with a westbound train in the Fall of 1967. Despite a number of newer EMD's, ALCO's and GE's, Pennsy's first generation power made a strong showing right up to the time Penn Central took over, with many of the PRR cab units surviving into Conrail. While PC put up with the F-units out of necessity, Conrail would not, striking them from the roster as soon as they could get along without them. The bridge in the background is the old overpass at 17th Street in Juniata which can be seen way in the background in the top photo on page 16, looking east from Juniata's 8th Street bridge.

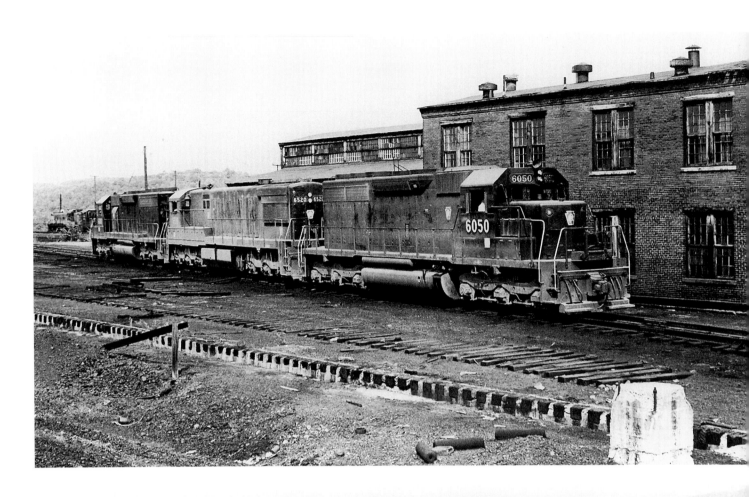

OPPOSITE ABOVE: Eighty-eight hundred potential horsepower in the form of two SD40's and a U28C prepare to leave the East Altoona locomotive terminal in 1967. Pennsylvania Railroad operated a decent fleet of General Electrics, but were outnumbered by the huge PRR armada of EMD's made up of F-units, Geeps and SD's. At this time, the SD40's were the newest EMD's running around the system.

OPPOSITE BELOW: A very busy scene from the Juniata 8th Street bridge shows a set of fast Penn Central power moving out, consisting of a GP38-2, a GP38, a GP40 and a C425. Another lashup in the background has a pair of GP38-2's and a GP30. SW7 #9072 is pulling company gons full of panel track and the yard is filled with a zillion cars, mostly owned by Penn Central. The 9072 seemingly had been in Altoona forever, from PRR and Penn Central days when it wore black, right up into the Conrail era when it wore blue and white.

ABOVE: Deep in the recesses of this man-made canyon, a crewmember fills a thirsty General Electric locomotive with water from a hose at Juniata's Rose Tower. It's much less glamorous than pulling up to a tank and swinging a spout to water your K-4 in the days of steam, but it is just as important today. Getting trains up and down the mountain generates a lot of heat, requiring a reliable supply of water to keep the engines cool. This interesting view gives you a good closeup look at the wire grates above the GE's radiators and the oval turbocharger stack.

OPPOSITE ABOVE: Here is just about the strangest lashup you'll ever see passing beneath the 8th St. bridge in Juniata. On the head end of this train is Penn Central U23B #2772, followed by Penn Central SD35 #6002, a Central Railroad of New Jersey SD40, an Erie Lackawanna SD45 and a Conrail first generation Geep followed by two Penn Central cabooses. The 2772 is actually running forward, as it is one of a group of U23B's purchased by Penn Central in 1973 with dual controls. Notice the stored power in the yard, including Erie Lackawanna switchers and the Tuscan and silver cab units. There is even a two-domed green tank car hiding in there! The silver bungalow on the left is CP-Homer and the signal facing you is number 2340 located near milepost 234. The double-masted signals are number 2341. The siding beneath the jade green boxcar is the old connection to the Altoona, Clearfield and Northern, which served Wopsononock Mountain resort and coalfields of Cambria county. The mainline switch and the track are no longer there.

OPPOSITE BELOW: In Fall of 1967 a pair of Pennsy big boats await their next assignment in the facility just west of Juniata's 8th Street bridge. The 6513 is a U25C and the 6532 is a later U28C. Notice the differences in the trucks, radiators, handrail arrangements, numbering styles and keystone placement. These early GE's could lug a good sized train, but they just weren't as reliable as SD40's. Conrail dumped most of their big U-Boats early in the game in favor of a fleet of 167 SD40-2's which they bought from 1977 to 1979 and numbered 6358-6524. Just behind the 6513 you can see a Tuscan Red passenger car in the storage yard.

ABOVE: Showing off her fresh paint, ALCO RSD12 class unit #6855 (delivered as PRR #8655) is poised for action at Altoona in 1968. This is one of 25 RSD12's ordered by Pennsy for pusher and transfer duty. After ten years of service it was pretty much a given that it would be relegated to yard duty; the last thing an operator needed was an ALCO failing on the hill... although I'll bet you could occasionally see one sneaking past Slope Tower!

The Pennsylvania Railroad in the Nuclear Age
Part I

In 1948 the Pennsylvania Railroad's Test Department opened a state of the art X-Ray Laboratory in Altoona. A 250,000 volt machine bombarded metal parts used to build cars and locomotives with radiation and checked them for strength and hidden defects that couldn't be seen with the naked eye.

BELOW: After years of faithful revenue service, PRR Express Messenger / Baggage Car type B-60b #9236 was photographed in the deadline at Juniata in spring 1971. Apparently Amtrak did not have a use for the 9236, so it was consigned to the scrapyard. The star designated Express Messenger service which meant that a rider would be working the car and sorting packages enroute. The vents on the roof and the porthole windows on the doors are concessions to the rider, along with a toilet. Forty of these cars were rebuilt from standard baggage cars by the Altoona Shops in 1964. Notice the rain gutters over the door openings to keep precious cargo from getting a shower from the rounded roof during loading and unloading.

OPPOSITE: Alongside the A&P warehouse, freshly painted GP7 #5876 is tugging a New York Central boxcar past a bright green Penn Central caboose, one of the ubiquitous Pennsy N5C's. Notice the unusual sign stenciled on the side of the GP7, with the initials "R.I." and what appears to be a four-digit road number. The 5876 is ex-PRR and is among the minority of GP7's having dynamic brakes. Later on in the day, former PRR RS27 #2406 and C425 #2432 rolled eastbound past the same location, photographed from the 4th Street footbridge at South Tower in Spring 1971. The A&P warehouse is actually owned by Ward Trucking, but was utilized by A&P at that time. Today there are big letters spelling out "Nabisco" on the side of it.

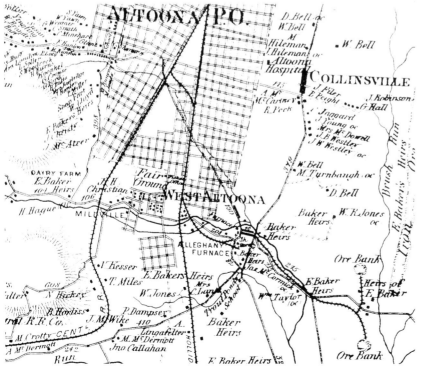

BOTH PAGES: Here's another GP7 with dynamic brakes -- Penn Central #5855 is pushing an ex-PRR cabin down the local freight tracks to tack it on the rear of a loaded eastbound coal train. Notice the "bowtie" snowplow, an indicator that this GP7 is used for more than local yard work. In the background are trailers lettered for Penn Central, Pennsylvania and New York Central and you can see the city of Altoona spreading out in the distance. Both photos were taken from the 4th Street pedestrian overpass near South Tower.

OPPOSITE ABOVE: PRR GP35 #2324, GP30 #2229, RS3 #5444, an SD35 and an unidentified EMD unit lead a mineral train west past South Tower on April 14, 1967. Notice the midtrain helpers just getting to the 4th Street footbridge. The tall stacks belong to the power plant of the Altoona Car Shops and the white building is a newer addition to the former Bolt Shop.

OPPOSITE BELOW: An SD35, a U25C and an SD40 push on the hind end of this same train on April 14, 1967. South Tower's location in the shadow of the pedestrian overpass is easily pinpointed in this photo. Today, the bridge is closed and the tower is gone.

The Pennsylvania Railroad in the Nuclear Age
Part II

The PRR experimented with nuclear switch-lamps installed at the PRR industrial siding at 19th Street & Margaret Avenue in 1958. These lamps used four bulbs that contained radioactive gas which reacted with a phosphorescent coating. They were visible from 1500 feet at night and glowed for ten years.

ABOVE: Smaller General Motors switchers flank six-axle brutes from GE and EMD idling side-by-side in the expansive Altoona Yards. The 6524 is a U28C built in 1966 and the 6181 is an SD45 built about a year later. It is 1969 and the Penn Central influence is slowly creeping into Altoona. New York Central hoppers surely have shown up several thousand times over the past decades, but the red "P" logo on the unit in the background is something new for the local crews to get used to.

OPPOSITE: Coming and going at Works Tower... boxcars, intermodal and a few passengers cars. Who said that the modern Amtrak "freights" are something new? Ironically, the passenger trains in Altoona today are looking a lot like Altoona's passenger trains of 1967... of course you are unlikely to find an E8 on the point or steam leaking from the rear coach! Pennsylvania Railroad E8A #4250 (ex-5790) has the honors on this June day. In the top photo, the building with the rounded tops on the two big doors is the Passenger Car Erecting Shop #1. The bottom photo shows a string of tank cars that need work done on them; they are parked along the Bolt Shop of the former Altoona Passenger Car Shops. The tank car repair facility is now owned by the Union Tank Car Company. SW7 #9072 is moving an ancient outside-braced wooden car in the distance. At this late date, the car is likely used by the maintenance department, rather than by valued paying customers. One of the oddest sights is the utility pole near the center of the photo that is practically being bent over by the support wires.

ABOVE: The Altoona shifter is passed by an eastbound TrucTrain at Works in June 1967. Fast intermodal trains have been polishing the rails of Middle Division for more than three decades, although containers now outnumber trailers. Lead unit U25C #6513 exhibits the early one-piece high-visibility windshield that soon lost favor due to its high replacement cost. Altoona is always busy and the overhead bridge at Works was a great place to catch the action. Under the 7th Street bridge in the distance, EMD helpers are assisting yet another westbound train up the mountain.

OPPOSITE ABOVE: The eastbound "Pennsylvania Limited" is accelerating away from the Altoona station behind three E's, with E7 #4201 (originally 5841) on the point. Notice the carloads of pipe (most likely from Bethlehem Steel's Steelton plant along the PRR near Harrisburg) moving out on the westbound freight which also includes classic Erie and Northern Pacific boxes. Beyond that train there is a power consist in the yard that includes an SD35, an RS3 and a GP30 -- an unusual sight, even in early 1967. The poor financial health of the Pennsy is evident by the new utilitarian paint scheme being applied to her passenger fleet. The building on the extreme left is the same warehouse shown earlier in this book with the A&P sign on it. At the time of this photo it sported the words "Ship Ward" high above the far side of the building.

OPPOSITE BELOW: A Penn Central SD40 and SD45 slither out of the Altoona yards with westbound freight in late winter 1970. This vantage point gives you a great look at the Passenger Car Erecting Shop #1 which features doors with the very unique rounded tops. This shop and the smaller grey building next to it are gone, and only one of the two smokestacks still exist. The big green building in the back is the Steel Shop and it is still there, in addition to the Tank Shop building, which is just to the left and hidden by the Erecting Shop. All of them are now painted brick red.

ABOVE: Early in 1969 was an interesting time to be in Altoona. Let's look around the yard from the 4th Street pedestrian over-pass and take some inventory. The empty coal train has a GP35 and a GP9 for power. The other set of power in the foreground is a pair of ALCO Century 630's still in pure Pennsy paint. There are heavyweight and stainless steel coaches on a siding and the yard is sprinkled with cars painted in cheery Penn Central green. I think I'll take the ALCO's for $200, Alex.

The Car Shops, or "Works" as it was also known, occupied over 60 acres at the turn of the century. The Passenger Car Shop could build 25 cars a month. The circular Freight Car Shop looked like a locomotive roundhouse. It was 433 feet in diameter with a 100-foot turntable in the center, and could build 75 cars under cover at one time. The Car Shops even had their own Fire Engine House with a steam fire engine and a hose carriage!

BELOW: In June 1967 a GP9, FP7 and an RS3 head over to the south side of the yard with a cut of cars that includes a PRR Fruit Growers Express insulated boxcar. In the distance, an RS11 burbles back west towards the 4th Street bridge. Notice the wooden freight shed and strings of reefers on the right side of the photo. There is even a silver Pennsy TrucTrain trailer beyond the FGEX reefer. You have got to give the Pennsy credit when it comes to interesting structures, like that classic light tower!

OPPOSITE: In 1967 a trio of EMD's have just descended the East Slope with a TrucTrain and are on the move eastbound towards Works Tower in downtown Altoona. This view gives you an excellent look at the back side of one of the stylish PRR position-light signals.

OPPOSITE ABOVE: As the crew of Penn Central GP35 #2293 climbs aboard in Spring 1971, it's worth walking across the foot-bridge and taking a look at some of the interesting equipment sitting around the yard. Check out those Pennsy RPO's, the D&H bright yellow and blue boxes and the two-bay coal hoppers -- not bad for an era when railfans complained about black Penn Central diesels! That Pennsy boxcar is a 40-foot RBL, an insulated car equipped with Evans "Quick Loader" fixtures to prevent damage to its lading. The "DF" stenciled on the door stands for "Damage Free". Note that the white paint on the PRR boxcar seems to be holding up much better than the white paint on the Penn Central GP35. Next to the yellow shed in the lower right hand corner, brakeshoes are stacked up in neat little piles. This is one commodity that you can bet on finding at the base of all mountain railroads.

OPPOSITE BELOW: Conrail #6373 is leading a mixed bag of General Electrics and EMD's on a westbound train past a string of CSX units at CP-Works in July 1992. This SD40-2 was painted in the Altoona shops for the United States Cycling Federation, who sponsored time trials in Altoona from June 11-21, 1992, for the 1992 Summer Olympics at Barcelona. The Olympic lettering was whited out in 1993 and the 6373 was repainted into the Conrail Quality scheme in 1995. On July 20, 1999, it became CSX 8803.

ABOVE: Pennsylvania Railroad GP35 #2315, RS27 #2411 and GP30 #2226 are preparing to assault the eastern face of the Alleghenies with a hopper train in late summer of 1966. There is now another highway bridge between the 7th Street bridge shown and where the locomotives are. Note that the two trailing units still have their Trainphone antennae. The two EMD's have boxes containing cab signal equipment on the engineer's walkway next to the nose that give them the flexibility to lead trains without restriction. The RS27 does not have a box for cab signals, allowing room for a keystone to be placed on the right side of its nose. Standard painting practice for the Pennsy in the Sixties placed keystones on the fireman's side of the nose on hood units, and those with cab signal boxes did not get one on the engineer's side of the nose.

BELOW: An ALCO Century 628 and an SD35 apply pressure to the back end of a westbound merchandise train rolling under the 7th Street bridge in Altoona in June 1967. Oddly enough, the SD35's didn't last much longer than the 628's! This photo was taken from near South Tower.

Towering behind the Penn Central SD45's on page 33, the Altoona Shops at 12th Street began to take shape in 1850. In five years they were a thousand feet long and were run by a thousand men. In 1870 separate car shops were opened, leaving the 12th Street Shops to handle locomotives. After a fire on December 27, 1931, locomotive work moved to Juniata and 12th Street concentrated on repairing cars and eventually diesel engines and traction motors.

OPPOSITE ABOVE: The fireman in Penn Central SD45 #6120 relaxes as he moves his eastbound Pennsylvania Power & Light coal train through Altoona; the hardest part of this trip is over. The relatively flat run toward Harrisburg will be a cakewalk compared to the descent of the East Slope. The PC worms are young and fresh in this Spring 1969 view and the 6217 is still in pure Pennsy paint. Those buildings looming over the train are part of the Altoona 12th Street Machine Shops. They are gone and the Station Mall is located there now. The Power House is at the right edge of the photo. Next to that are the Diesel Repair Shop, the Fabricating Shops and the Truck Shop.

OPPOSITE BELOW: An assortment of early first generation power is dragging an eastbound mixed freight through Altoona in early Summer 1966. The "handrails" on top of the F-units and the trailing Geep are actually part of the PRR train telephone system, which was developed jointly by the Pennsy, Union Switch & Signal and General Electric. This system utilized high frequency alternating electric currents that were transmitted by induction to the rails and existing wires along the PRR right of way. Notice the old station and the baggage carts on the right side of the picture. From this perch on the pedestrian walkway, you also get a good overview of the Altoona Machine Shops. You won't see these shops, the old station or even the "modern" Wolf Office Center anymore. If those baggage carts would be there today they would be run over by speeding automobiles on the "PRR Expressway" shown on page 37.

Here are three views of westbound Train #23 the "Manhattan Limited" rolling to a stop in front of the Altoona Passenger Station in May 1969. E8 #4309 (originally #5895) is in charge of today's consist. Two views are from the pedestrian footbridge; note the eastbound piggyback train with trailers from CB&Q, Illinois Central, PRR and Penn Central rolling along the high iron. The third view is from farther west along the platform. Notice how shiny the grilles on the 4309 look from above, but appear completely different on the ground level view! Passenger service at the end of the decade is showing signs of decay -- tired E-units, a crumbling platform and litter on the ground -- however, once the train is loaded, #23 will make an on-time departure at 7:57 pm. The two-story brick building on the left is the freight station, housing the Railway Express Agency. The Altoona Post Office is conveniently located between this building and the passenger station.

Altoona's passenger service started out very modestly in a small frame structure on 9th Avenue at 12th Street. On February 15, 1854, a two-story brick station at 10th Ave. and 13th St. opened to coincide with the completion of the mainline via Horseshoe Curve. The station that served Altoona for almost a century was built on the same site in 1887. After years using a temporary trailer, passengers are now served by the Altoona Transportation Center.

According to "The City of Altoona, Pennsylvania, A.D. 1896", The Pennsylvania Railroad carried 60,472,252 passengers in 1894 for an average distance of 18 miles! Twelve daily passenger trains went west from Altoona, eleven went east and six went south.

BELOW: The power of this smart looking westbound train is at the eastern edge of the passenger platform in late Summer 1966. Three matching black and gold F-units, led by F3A #9528, are about to depart Altoona with an early intermodal train. The piggyback boom did not take place until the 1970's and '80's, but the Pennsy was already running long TrucTrains over the Alleghenies in the 1960's. Penn Central introduced the New York Central's Flexi-Van and Super-Van names to former-PRR salespeople in 1968 and changed to TrailVan trains during the next decade, perhaps to quell fighting between the Red and Green teams. This nomenclature remained to the end of Conrail, earning intermodal movements the popular moniker "TV trains". It was an easy symbol to remember and astute dispatchers knew better than to delay a TV train.

OPPOSITE ABOVE: A four-unit helper set consisting of SD40-2's numbered 6390, 6384, 6366 and 6378 rolls beneath the westbound signal bridge at Alto interlocking on the Ides of March, 1997. The photo is taken from the 17th Street bridge and you can see the old Wolf Furniture Office Center which is no longer there. The concrete tower with the letter "a" is the Altoona Transportation Center, hosting Amtrak trains, Amtran buses (local) and Greyhound. The road to the left of the railroad has been renamed the "PRR Expressway" according to a street sign at the station.

OPPOSITE BELOW: Amtrak's Train #40, the eastbound "Broadway Limited", is cruising by Alto Tower on January 26, 1993. Led by F40PH's #297 and #219, the first half of this Chicago to New York train consists of Material Handling Cars. This photo was taken from the 17th Street bridge.

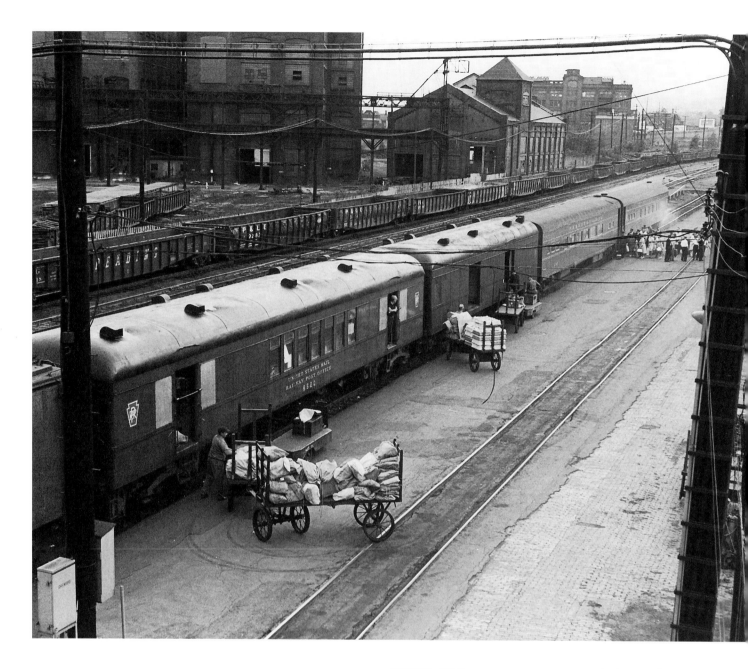

1154-A12. (Allgy. & Pgh. Div.). Passenger trainmen, and attendant must keep the doors of toilet rooms in passenger equipment locked at Altoona, and between Wilkinsburg and Pittsburgh.

From the Penn Central Central Region Timetable #1
In effect 4:01A.M., Sunday, April 28, 1968

ABOVE: While passengers are escorted onto the eastbound "Juniata" further down the platform, an Express Messenger car is worked by PRR personnel while an RPO is taken care of by Altoona Post Office employees in this interesting 1967 overhead view. The loaded carts are quickly emptied, and the train is soon filled. Modern-day visitors to Altoona can shop at the Station Mall and eat at the McDonalds which are now located where the Machine Shops appear in this photo. The building along the tracks is the Power Plant, and then looking to the left is the Diesel Engine Repair Shop and the Fabricating Shops. The large building in the background is the Test Plant.

OPPOSITE: It takes more than engineers and dispatchers to keep trains moving across the PRR. Railroaders in work-clothes and uniformed trainmen prepare to add cars to the end of the westbound "Juniata" at the Altoona Station platform.

BELOW: At CP-Slope, two GP40's led by Conrail #3154 prepare to make a frontal assault on the Allegheny Mountains in late Summer 1980. With only eight axles and six thousand horses up front, you can bet that this train has helpers shoving on the rear! The track layout has since changed; the eastbound signal indicating a red "stop" is no longer on this signal bridge today, but two dwarf signals were added near the signal bridge. Also, a signal mast for eastbound trains was added east of this signa! bridge between tracks one and two.

RIGHT: Current track layout looking east from 24-1/2 Street bridge. July 18, 2000. Photo by Jaime F.M. Serensits.

OPPOSITE ABOVE: Looking west from the 17th Street bridge, four SD45's are waiting for trains to push over the mountain. The signal bridge is the eastbound home signal for Alto Tower. In the distance you can also see the signal bridge controlling Slope interlocking and a headlight peering through the haze. The hopper set out on the left appears to be a PP&L load. All six tracks are still there today and the signal bridge is painted silver.

OPPOSITE BELOW: Along 10th Street just east of Slope, a pair of crewmembers take a keen interest in the coupling of the SD40 helper to the rear of a westbound freight during the Summer of 1974. Despite the enormous volume of traffic that has been sent over the mountains west of Altoona, careful work by skilled crews have resulted in a very smooth operation with a phenomenal safety record. This is especially amazing when you consider that the weeds growing up on this important Penn Central mainline look like they belong on the branchline heading to Petticoat Junction. When you look at today's finely engineered mainlines, its hard to believe that this was what big-time railroading looked like in the Northeast only 25 years ago! Mercifully, Conrail was only two years away.

BELOW: With the assistance of a Clark tow motor, baggage carts loaded with express packages are flying all over the platform in perfect synchronicity as this Penn Central train is being worked at the Altoona Station in May 1969. This is one of the Express Messenger cars marked by the white star rebuilt by the Altoona Shops in '64. Amtrak has breathed new life into the railroad express business, although they certainly do not have employees riding in their express rolling stock! Today the buzz words are Material Handling Cars and RoadRailers.

OPPOSITE ABOVE: A couple of crewmembers hop aboard GP40-2 #3333 and prepare to assault the Allegheny Mountains. To say this TV train is overpowered would be an understatement... even for these tough grades! The mainline is flanked by Altoona's temporary Amtrak station on one side and the Altoona Pipe & Steel Supply Company on the other. Note the LEF&C boxcar at the loading dock. The Lake Erie, Franklin & Clarion is a shortline located in northwest Pennsylvania coal country. This is one of the old 12th Street Shop buildings (Erecting Shop #3) that has survived to today. The Altoona Railroader's Memorial Museum is housed in the old Master Mechanics building, which has been restored beautifully.

OPPOSITE BELOW: Altoona, Pennsylvania -- where The Central of New Jersey meets the Erie Lackawanna. Anyone who has spent any time in Altoona recognizes this location. This is a pair of helpers waiting near Alto Tower for the next train to go west. Regular helper power for many years consisted of a fleet of CNJ SD40's and Erie Lackawanna SD45's, SD45-2's and SDP45's. If you were anywhere else in the United States, seeing a combination of ex-CNJ and ex-EL units together on a freight train would have been quite unusual in 1987, but at Altoona it was an everyday occurrence. The large green Wolf Furniture building has been a fixture for many years on 11th Street in Altoona. It is on the site of the original Wolf Furniture store which housed the corporate headquarters even after the retail store was closed in the early 1980's. The new store is out of the downtown area off of Plank Road. The familiar green facing you have seen in many photos taken near Alto Tower was added when the store was remodeled and air conditioned. In 1998 the building was razed and the beautiful Charles E. Wolf Court retirement home was built where this building once stood. Photo by Jaime F. M. Serensits.

OPPOSITE ABOVE: It's close to noon, and Pennsy E7 #4210 (originally 5850) and three other E-units are in charge of the eastbound "Pennsylvania Limited" passing Slope Tower in July 1966 with a healthy consist of express boxcars. (Slope Tower was formerly called BO Tower -- the modern BO Tower is in Kalamazoo where the Grand Rapids & Indiana crossed the Michigan Central. In Penn Central days it was located along the Buffalo to Chicago mainline and controlled the CK&S Branch, Kalamazoo Branch, GR&I Branch, GTW Ry. Crossing and South Haven Branch. The tower was named for nearby Botsford Yard.) The eastbound and westbound interlocking signals for Slope are visible in this photo, along with the 24th Street bridge and the roof of Slope Tower. The bridge was later rebuilt just west of its original location and is referred to as the 24-1/2 Street bridge by some sources. In the field at the left, PRR had constructed locomotive servicing facilities to coal and water helpers in between assignments without having to bring the locomotives into town, along with their accompanying soot and noise. This facility included a 75-foot turntable to turn steam locomotives.

OPPOSITE BELOW: How's this for a consist? A pair of ALCO C628's in basic black and three Tuscan E's power a long westbound Train 23 and 43, the "Manhattan Limited" between Alto and Slope interlocking towers during the summer of 1966. The big ALCO's were added in Altoona to insure that gravity would not hinder this hot train as it crossed the Alleghenies. Residents of these houses on 10th Street have a bird's eye view of the action on the PRR mainline.

ABOVE: A second set of six-axle helpers tie onto the rear end of this westbound iron ore train in late summer of 1972. The iron ore is heavy, so it does not get loaded very high in the cars. Had this been an empty hopper train going back to the mines, a second helper set surely would not have been necessary. The ore movements were some of the heaviest trains run over the Alleghenies, often receiving midtrain helpers, as well as pushers on the back end. The green bay window caboose will be sandwiched between thousands of tons of ore and the 13,800 horsepower provided by three SD45's and an SD40 (6231-6175-6211-6052). The signal bridge is the eastbound home signal for aptly-named Slope interlocking.

OPPOSITE ABOVE: Mr. Hatfield visits Mr. McCoy. The New York Central sleeper "La Porte County", looking very much out of place on the Broad Way of Commerce, brings up the markers of an eastbound "Pennsylvania Limited" in 1967. Ironically, the Pennsy mainline from Fort Wayne to Chicago traverses the southwest portion of La Porte County in Indiana! The head end of the train is at Alto and nearing the Altoona Station. In order to get the train on the proper station track, the Limited is on a track normally reserved for westbound movements.

OPPOSITE BELOW: Two General Motors SD35's and an ALCO Century 628 are running light towards downtown Altoona -- that's Slope Tower in the background. Westbound traffic must be heavier at this time of day, since the big helper set was not held for an eastbounder. Notice that the siding on the south side of the tracks comes to an end east of Slope's home signal.

ABOVE: With the sun in his eyes, the hogger notches up his trio of EMD's as he climbs out of Altoona with a long mixed freight. In the background you can see the eastbound signal bridge belonging to Slope interlocking and another set of power beneath it on the far track. The black paint remains, but Penn Central's friendly worms have replaced Pennsy keystones on all of the motive power in this scene.

OPPOSITE ABOVE: On August 25, 1981, Conrail GP40 #3230, GP35 #2358, SD45 #6137 and a pup are under way with a puff of dark smoke and are heading west beneath the 24th Street bridge with the city of Altoona in the background. You can barely see the Slope interlocking box through the Penn Central open bilevel autorack. The new "24-1/2 Street" bridge has an 8-foot chainlink fence on the east side.

OPPOSITE BELOW: A Pennsy cabin trails a long string of express cars making their way up the eastern slope of the Allegheny Mountains in the Summer of 1966. Although the train is barely out of Altoona, you can bet that this hot express train is over-powered and rocketing up the hill behind that long string of E-units on the head end. It's easy to see the stiff grade that lies ahead when you look at the tracks in front of the train.

ABOVE: F7 #9768, a Geep and another F-unit are easing their 78-car train through Slope interlocking on August 19, 1964. If you look closely you can see the Brick Yard in the background and another eastbound waiting for this train to crossover and clear the interlocking. The westbound signal is numbered 2373, while the eastbound signals on this bridge are home signals controlling the Slope interlocking plant. Today the track that this train is crossing over from is gone, and the signal bridge no longer has eastbound or westbound signals for track three. This deep cut is indicative of how difficult it must have been to build a railroad over the Alleghenies... and this is just the foot of the mountain! Photograph by Kenneth M. Ardinger.

BELOW: Conrail SD40-2 #6471 and three GE's blast their way up the hill west of CP-Slope with a westbound TV train in late summer 1994. The power has just encountered the sag in the hill and they are pouring it on as they pass a slower grain train struggling up the mountain on track 3. You can see the signal bridges on both sides of the 24th Street bridge in the distance.

OPPOSITE ABOVE: On July 16, 1983, an ex-EL SDP45 splits a pair of SD45-2's next to the Brick Yard at Coburn, with the city of Altoona nestled in the valley beyond. After Erie Lackawanna was folded into Conrail, these big 20-cylinder units spent many years around Altoona helping trains up and down the hill. Notice the switch into the Brick Yard just ahead of the first unit.

OPPOSITE BELOW: How many places could you witness this scene in the 1990's? In September 1997, Amtrak's "Pennsylvanian" is rolling downgrade through the man-made canyon whose walls consist of a Conrail mixed freight powered by SD40-2 #6459 and Southern Pacific SD40T-2 #8322, and a Triple Crown RoadRailer. These trains are occupying all three tracks adjacent to the Brick Yard at Coburn, just west of Slope. The famous "Brick Yard" visible on the right side of the photo is officially the Altoona Plant of Premier Refractories International.

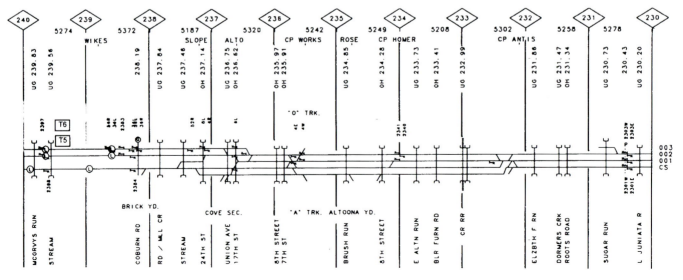

PREVIOUS PAGES: Here's a sight and sound you are not likely to forget -- 6547, 6529 and 6533 -- a U33C/U28C/U28C combination lugging a loaded ore train up to the top of the Allegheny Mountains. There was also an SD45 and three SD40's shoving on the hind end for good measure! These four views were taken at Scotch Run (Official Conrail documents call this Scotts Run) below Horseshoe Curve in Conrail's younger days. The signal bridge is number 2406/7.

OPPOSITE ABOVE: The brakeshoe smoke from this heavy train has created a blue haze which seems to perpetually cover the East Slope. In late Fall 1967, Pennsylvania Railroad #6169 and another SD45 are holding back an eastbound merchandise train at the site of old GY Tower, several miles below Horseshoe Curve. GY Tower was the first interlocking plant built between Altoona and Gallitzin and named for nearby McGarveys Run. The front end of the train has already rounded Wikes Curve in the distance, while McGarveys Curve is just west of here. Notice how the rock face has been notched to make room for the north leg of Signal Bridge 2398.

OPPOSITE BELOW: Former EL SD45-2 #6665 and a Penn Central SD40 march down the East Slope of the Alleghenies while the rear of their train is on the far side of the valley, having not yet negotiated Horseshoe Curve. There is a good snow cover and the sun is shining on February 11, 1977. The tunnel that provides passage for a road and Glenwhite Run (named for a Baltimore coal company that had a branch leaving the PRR mainline right from Horseshoe Curve!) is easily seen on the right from this elevated perch near the former location of Kittanning Point station.

ABOVE: A long westbound Conrail freight approaches the signal bridge just below Horseshoe Curve. The snow cover and bare trees present a perfect opportunity to see the foundation of the old water tank on the hillside east of the Kittanning Point station site and the old roadbed of the track that carried coal to overhead coaling tracks. Yes, steam engines were coaled and watered on the mountain just east of Horseshoe Curve! If you look very closely, you will notice that there is a still a red keystone visible on the second SD40.

BELOW: In 1981, a pair of elderly ex-Erie Lackawanna GP35's and a newer bought-by-Conrail SD40-2 have a hot, hot, hot train loaded with finished automobiles and auto parts blasting their way up the hill at Scotch Run. This was during the era before enclosed trilevels, which was a time that automobile trains were much more interesting. Signal bridge 2406 is the second set of signals an eastbound freight encounters after negotiating Horseshoe Curve.

OPPOSITE ABOVE: A PRR westbound freight headed by new F3 #9530 continues to climb the East Slope on June 26, 1950. The 9530's clean lines can be attributed to a coupler shroud and the absence of m.u. cables. The clean lines of the railroad right of way can be attributed to impeccable PRR maintenance standards; in 1950 the Pennsylvania Railroad was a good looking road that took a lot of pride in its appearance. Signal bridge 2416 is just below Horseshoe Curve near the old Kittanning Point station. Notice the standpipes where steam locomotives were watered and also loaded with coal here. The foundation of the old water tank is visible in the color photograph on page 55. Photo by William P. Price, collection of Thomas A. Biery.

OPPOSITE BELOW: ALCO's are outnumbering EMD's three to two on this westbound freight photographed on May 6, 1972. The hot eastbound merchandise train swinging around the Curve features fifteen shiny new automobiles on a single open trilevel car -- a far cry from today's completely enclosed multilevels.

BELOW: In late Summer 1972 a westbound TrailVan train grinds uphill on a straightaway below Horseshoe Curve. This eclectic consist includes three E-units, a GP35 and a U30B with two SD45's helping on the head end. Notice the telephone box in the distance and the buckets of spikes lying all along the tracks. Despite the low maintenance standards that Penn Central was famous for in the 1970's, all but track one is welded and the spikes show at least an effort on PC management's part to keep this vital mainline fluid. Considering that today's priority intermodal trains get the latest and greatest power, it is pretty amazing to see these 20-year old cab units on such a hot train!

OPPOSITE ABOVE: During the first few years of Conrail's existence, it was common to see all types of power running anywhere on the system. Here we see an Erie Lackawanna SD45 leading Penn Central, Central Railroad of New Jersey and Conrail units approaching signal bridge 2417 (2416 on the side facing the train) on February 11, 1977. The train consists mostly of midwest traffic, including boxcars from Illinois Central Gulf, Rock Island, Gulf, Mobile & Ohio and Union Pacific. As years moved on, Conrail retired all of their gas-guzzling SD45's relatively early, yet kept EL SDP45's and newer SD45-2's in Altoona helper service for over a decade.

OPPOSITE BELOW: "Pigs" ride the rails around Horseshoe Curve, courtesy of this westbound Conrail TV train on a snowy February 11, 1977. Power includes an Erie Lackawanna '45 and a Reading GP30. Notice that PRR 4-6-2 #1361 is in the park, but there is nobody visiting her on this cold February day. The K-4 would be replaced by Pennsy GP9 #7048 on September 16, 1985, courtesy of Conrail. The GP9 that replaced it on the Curve had to be repainted back into the Pennsylvania Railroad scheme from the Conrail blue & white it wore at the time it was donated.

In addition to the variety of motive power that has marched up and down the East Slope of the Alleghenies, an even greater number of freight cars have made the same trek. The wide open vista and slow speeds on the Curve make it a natural place to capture freight car roster shots as well as locomotive photos. Here are two examples of some of the gems we have found hiding in the middle of freight consists.

BELOW: Do you have a set of old Mirro Craft kitchen accessories? If so, your cookware may have been riding in spectacular fashion around Horseshoe Curve in 1978! This insulated boxcar was leased to Mirro Craft by the Chicago Freight Car Leasing Company. This car is equipped with DF-2 (Damage-Free) Loaders which lock the product in place in the car to keep the load safe and secure while in transit.

OPPOSITE: More than twenty years after Conrail folded 6 bankrupt carriers together, you could still see vestiges of the old railroads. Here is a trio of three-bay Erie Lackawanna hoppers that haven't even been given a new set of reporting marks or numbers, looking just like they did when they rolled out of the shops in April 1974, albeit a little worse for wear. It is the Summer of 1996 and these cars make for a nice sight as they parade uphill to the delight of the visitors at the Horseshoe Curve park. Photo by Jaime F. M. Serensits.

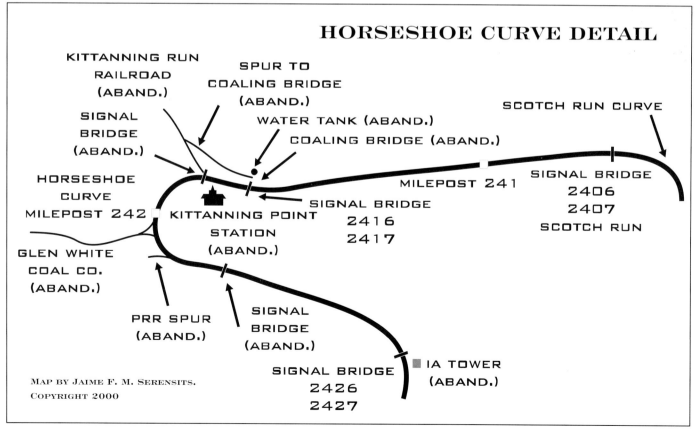

HORSESHOE CURVE DETAIL

KITTANNING RUN
RAILROAD
(ABAND.)

SPUR TO
COALING BRIDGE
(ABAND.)

SCOTCH RUN CURVE

SIGNAL
BRIDGE
(ABAND.)

WATER TANK (ABAND.)

COALING BRIDGE (ABAND.)

HORSESHOE
CURVE
MILEPOST 242

MILEPOST 241

SIGNAL BRIDGE
2406
2407
SCOTCH RUN

KITTANNING POINT
STATION
(ABAND.)

SIGNAL BRIDGE
2416
2417

GLEN WHITE
COAL CO.
(ABAND.)

PRR SPUR
(ABAND.)

SIGNAL
BRIDGE
(ABAND.)

SIGNAL BRIDGE
2426
2427

IA TOWER
(ABAND.)

MAP BY JAIME F. M. SERENSITS.
COPYRIGHT 2000

OPPOSITE ABOVE: You can already hear the flanges squealing on the long 89-foot flats as Conrail SD50 #6776 and GP40-2 #3331 lumber into view with a westbound trailer train featuring a Southern Pacific "Golden Pig" at the front of the consist. This is the view from the park at Horseshoe Curve on October 29, 1988. Camouflaged among the muted fall colors, signal bridge 2416 is barely visible beyond the trees on the right. Photo by Jaime F.M. Serensits.

OPPOSITE BELOW: Penn Central caboose #23091 is on the rear of a Pennsylvania Power & Light coal train turning the corner at Horseshoe in September 1973. The paint is a almost a perfect match of the crewmember's work clothes! He's watching his train from the inside of the curve to look for any defects that could lead to disaster on the steep descent. Notice the absence of the PC "worms" logo, the gold color of the lettering and numbering and the presence of an ACI tag. Also, look at how high the step is to get up on the caboose! This N5C is a former PRR cabin noted for its round "porthole" windows.

ABOVE: All in the 35 family. PRR SD35's #6027, #6020 and freshly painted GP35 #2273 are in full dynamic as they head east around the park at Horseshoe Curve. Note the New York Central and Delaware & Hudson boxcars on this overcast April 14, 1967, scene. The 6020 is one of the SD35's that would later acquire a red "P" logo as Penn Central attempted to dress up their paint scheme.

The Horseshoe Curve was more than a place that the PRR mainline changed direction and gained altitude. It was the home for a passenger station called Kittanning Point, site of a coaling and watering station and the point at which two branchlines headed out into the wilderness. The Kittanning Run Railroad was built toward Coupon and served the mines of S.E. Baker. Another branch served the Baltimore Coal & Lumber Co. mine beyond Glen White. Although these mines seemed to be out in the middle of nowhere, the town of Glen White had its own post office and sawmill.

OPPOSITE ABOVE: Adding a splash of color to the Alleghenies, Lehigh Valley U23B #503 makes an appearance on Horseshoe Curve, squeezed in between Penn Central SD45 #6195 and U23B #2718. It didn't take Conrail long to begin shuffling its motive power around, since this photo was taken on May 22, 1976, just a few weeks after Conrail was formed. The Lehigh Valley was one of the smaller roads absorbed by Conrail. It started as a proud anthracite carrier and evolved into a transcontinental connection for intermodal trains interchanged with the Norfolk & Western at Buffalo, New York. PRR acquired controlling interest in the LVRR in 1962, so when it was folded into Consolidated Rail Corporation, it was actually a subsidiary of Penn Central at the time.

OPPOSITE BELOW: Penn Central GP38-2 #8117 loops its merchandise around 4-6-2 #1361 displayed at the Horseshoe Curve on June 25, 1977. In September 1985, PRR GP9 #7048 would replace the 1361, which was restored to operating condition and pulled excursions on PRR mainlines, including this one. Notice also the red, white and blue trash barrels in the park, a remnant from the previous year's bicentennial celebration.

ABOVE: A former Penn Central SD40, an ex-CNJ SD40 and a Conrail-bought SD40-2 have an eastbound mixed freight rolling downhill around the location of the old Kittanning Point station complex. The old grade of the spur which brought coal down to Pennsy's overhead coal bridge is easily discernable on the hil!side above the 6301. This spur branched off the Kittanning Run Railroad, which interchanged traffic with the PRR just west of here on the Curve. This small railroad ran to the S.E. Baker mines just north of here. In early days loaded cars were allowed to roll freely downhill from these mines without the assistance of a locomotive!

It is a cold and cloudy March 1977 weekend at Horseshoe Curve. Our vantage point for these two views is an outcrop of rock west of the visitor center and high above the Altoona Water Supply. A blue Conrail E8 #4022 (ex-ERIE #833, built in March 1951) is leading Amtrak's "National Limited" downgrade and east to New York. The four-track mainline appears again in the distance above the access road and the Altoona Water Works sign. Catching the 4022 on this train was very lucky, for this is the first E8 Conrail assigned to its own executive train and was eventually painted dark green. It was later joined by 4020 and 4021 (ex-PRR #5809/PC 4309/AMTK 315/498 blt. 1/51 and ex-PRR #5711/PC 4311/AMTK 317/499 blt. 10/52). In this photo it is still blue, and was the only E8 ever painted in blue and white with full Conrail markings. Conrail later added black paint on the top of the nose and around the cab windows to reduce glare from the sun. The 4022 also received an air whistle to replace these standard airhorns. Notice the bug screen above the headlights!

1154-A14. (Allegheny Div.). On through passenger trains passing Horse Shoe Curve in daylight train crews will keep a lookout when approaching the curve and if they find that the view will be unobstructed the following announcement will be made:

WESTWARD:--"Attention please, we are now approaching the famous Horse Shoe Curve. View can be had from the left side of the car."

EASTWARD:--"Attention please, we are now approaching the famous Horse Shoe Curve. View can be had from the right side of the car."

These announcements should be made in all cars occupied by passengers, except private and business cars.

When a passenger train overtakes a moving train on a parallel track, the passenger train will not pass the train until the latter passes around the curve, if the passengers' view will be obscured by the train.

A passenger train meeting a moving train that will obscure the passengers' view will move slowly until the train has passed.

To comply with these instructions, enginemen will not delay their trains to exceed three minutes.

From the Penn Central Central Region Timetable #1
In effect 4:01A.M., Sunday, April 28, 1968

OPPOSITE ABOVE: You can see the entire MG interlocking plant in this view of Conrail SD40-2 #6483 and SD45 #6218 hauling a westbound freight up the hill on August 29, 1981. The lack of number plates on the bridge indicate absolute signals which govern the MG interlocking plant. Notice the missing section of the old track 2.

OPPOSITE BELOW: Sporting an unusual color for a Conrail revenue boxcar, number 360610 is photographed on a westbound freight near MG Tower on August 29, 1981. The 360610 is a former Erie Lackawanna RBL reefer. An RBL is an insulated boxcar with built-in devices used to reduce damage in transit, the bane of shippers and carriers. Boxcars with this feature are also known as "equipped" cars. Most of Conrail's freight car fleet received a coat of boxcar red, making this a very unusual sighting.

ABOVE: Those black GP38-2's seemed to be everywhere on Conrail in the very early 1980's, so it's not unusual to see a quartet of them pushing a train past MG Tower on August 29, 1981. What IS unusual is the "CONRAIL" name slapped across the black nose of 8074 -- this was definitely not standard practice. Most Penn Central units received only a "CR" stenciled on their nose in either standard "Conrail" or "Penn Central" style. This may not be the most photogenic consist in this book, but it's still part of the history of this region.

OPPOSITE ABOVE: Conrail SD40-2 #6360 grinds uphill past MG Tower with an empty hopper train in early 1987. This beautiful brick tower was built in 1944 to handle the incredible volume of traffic that moved over the hill during World War II. The MG interlocking plant consisted of a complete set of eastbound and westbound crossovers that had once been located at the former site of AG Tower further up the mountain. As part of a track rationalization program, Conrail removed one of the four tracks in front of the tower and decommissioned MG, as well. Photo by Jaime F. M. Serensits.

OPPOSITE BELOW: A caboose hop powered by GP38 #7832 and GP38-2's #8123 and #8147 have just passed MG Tower on their way west. Notice that a good chunk of track two is missing. The 7832 is passing over a track lubricator on track four, preparing it for the twists and turns between here and Bennington. Once track two is completely removed, the farthest track will be known as track three.

BELOW: An American Locomotive Company C425 and a General Electric U30B are climbing west of MG Tower in 1968. Although Pennsy and New York Central both preferred EMD products, most of the ALCO's and GE's inherited by Penn Central remained on the roster right up to the demise of PC in 1976. Notice that it is the GE, not the ALCO, which is sending a tall column of smoke up into the air.

OPPOSITE ABOVE: Conrail GP35 #3635 is leading a handful of former Penn Central GE's downhill on track 1 on March 27, 1977. The former Reading GP35's in this series were unique in that they were not renumbered when folded into the Conrail system. The silver box beneath the engineer's window contains cab signal equipment that allows this Reading unit to lead in PRR cab signal territory. As the consist swings around AG curve, MG Tower will be in sight of the engineer and fireman. Note the bracing in the side of the hill to prevent the tracks and the train from sliding down into Sugar Run. The trackage visible in the background across the ravine is the New Portage Secondary, and Muleshoe Curve is geographically southwest of here. The new US 22 alignment roughly follows the New Portage Secondary in this area.

OPPOSITE BELOW: Two Penn Central GP35's and a straight GP38 are heading uphill toward signal bridge 2444 at the previous site of AG Tower on March 27, 1977. Note the stone building on the left side of the tracks remaining from PRR days of old. This still is rugged country today, populated mainly by freight and passenger trains on this side of the valley and trucks and automobiles cruising up and down US 22 on the other side.

ABOVE: Penn Central SD45 #6229 is eastbound at AG, just west of the stone building. The train is on track 2 and the date is March 27, 1977. AG Tower and its associated crossovers were located just east of here, yet the "town" of Allegrippus was located farther west, not far from where the boxcars are clinging to the hillside in the background. It was a mining town that had a railroad station, as seen on the early map shown on page 77, and many of its residents likely worked at Bennington Furnace at one time or another, or may have participated in building one of the nearby tunnels. According to an 1895 atlas, Allegrippus did not have a post office, but it had an express office.

WHY THEY BUILT MG

New York, Philadelphia, Baltimore and Washington to Pittsburgh

PENNSYLVANIA R. R.

Lv. Boston, Mass. (N.Y.N.H.&H.) ... 11p55 11p55
Ar. New York, N. Y. (Penna. Sta.) ... 5 40 5 40

For additional Stops, consult local time tables.

For Sleeping, Parlor and Dining Cars, see pages 17 and 18.

(Eastern Standard Time.)

Train names (left to right): The Metropolitan (25) · The Duquesne (19) · The St. Louisan (33) · Pennsylvania Limited (5) · The Admiral (71) · The General (49) · The Red Arrow (69) · Cincinnati Limited (41) · Liberty Limited (59) · The Trail Blazer All-Coach Train (77) · Broadway Limited (29) · "Spirit of St. Louis" (31) · The Jeffersonian All-Coach Train (65) · "Spirit of St. Louis" (21) · Manhattan Limited (23) · The American (67) · The Clevelander (39) · The Akronite (9) · Pittsburgh Night Express (35) · Pittsburgh Night Express (661) · Iron City Express (37) · The Statesman (51) · The Golden Arrow (79) · The Golden Arrow (661) · The Pittsburgher (61)

(All trains Daily)

Principal timings (selected):

Lv. New York, N. Y. (Penna. Sta.) .... Dist. .0
Ar. Pittsburgh, Pa. (Penna. Sta.) .... Dist. 439.3

Distances (miles): New York 0 · Newark 10.0 · Elizabeth 15.5 · New Brunswick 32.7 · Trenton 58.1 · Philadelphia 85.9 · North Phila. 85.9 · Broad Street Station 91.4 · Penna. Station (30th Street) 91.4 · Paoli 111.4 · Downingtown 124.0 · Coatesville 130.0 · Parkesburg 135.7 · Lancaster 159.3 · Mount Joy 170.8 · Elizabethtown 177.6 · Middletown 185.1 · Harrisburg 194.6

Washington, D. C. .0 · Baltimore, Md. (Penna. Sta.) 40.1 · York 96.3 · Harrisburg 123.4

Harrisburg 194.6 · Duncannon 209.4 · Newport 222.0 · Mifflin 243.6 · Lewistown 255.2 · Mount Union 279.7 · Huntingdon 291.6 · Tyrone 311.2 · Altoona 325.4 · Cresson 339.9 · Johnstown 362.9 · Torrance 387.0 · Derry 394.3 · Latrobe 399.2 · Greensburg 408.5 · Jeannette 412.6 · Irwin 417.9 · Wilmerding 425.5 · East Pittsburgh 427.1 · Braddock 429.2 · Wilkinsburg 432.7 · East Liberty 434.7 · Pittsburgh 439.3

Notes:

* Daily.

† Daily except Sundays.

▲ On Sundays leaves Hudson Terminal 5.50 P. M., Jersey City 5.53 P. M.

♣ On Sundays leaves Hudson Terminal 5.40 P. M., Jersey City 5.43 P. M.

\# On Sundays, arrives 11.10 P. M.

⊕ Shuttle train from Broad St. Station, connecting with No. 25 at Penna. Station (30th St.).

b Stops only on notice to conductor to discharge passengers.

c Stops only to receive passengers.

d Stops only to discharge passengers.

e Stops Sundays only.

f Stops only on signal or notice to agent or conductor to receive or discharge passengers.

i No. 51, Washington to Harrisburg, leaves Harrisburg 2.18 A. M., arrives Altoona 4.48 A. M.

n Stops only to receive passengers for Altoona and beyond.

p Runs to Philadelphia, leaving New York 6.00 A. M., arriving Philadelphia, Broad Street Station 7.55 A. M.

q Stops only to receive passengers for Pittsburgh and beyond.

s Stops Sundays only on signal or notice to agent or conductor to receive or discharge passengers.

t Stops only to receive passengers for points west of Pittsburgh.

u Hudson & Manhattan R. R. Station.

v Stops only to receive passengers for points west of Philadelphia.

w No baggage service New York to Philadelphia.

x No baggage handled at this station.

y Passengers from New York change cars at Penna. Station (30th Street)

This is a June 20, 1943, PRR passenger timetable showing the scheduled trains. Remember that this does not include 2nd or 3rd sections, troop trains, or other extras. It also does not include scheduled freight trains or wartime extras for the

TOWER IN 1944

Pittsburgh to Baltimore, Washington, Philadelphia and New York

	The Jeffersonian All-Coach Train	The Pennsylvanian	The Rainbow	Pennsylvania Limited	The St. Louisan		Gotham Limited	The Juniata		The Duquesne	The New Englander	Mail	The New Yorker	Manhattan Limited	Philadelphia Express	Iron City Express		The Statesman	The American	The Pittsburgher	The Clevelander The Akronite	Philadelphia Night Express	The Admiral	Cincinnati Limited	The Red Arrow	The General	Liberty Limited	Broadway Limited	"Spirit of St. Louis"	The Trail Blazer All-Coach Train	"Spirit of St. Louis"
(For additional stops consult local time tables. For Sleeping, Parlor and Dining Cars, see pages 18 to 20)	64	78	42	2	32	8	54	72	24	74	46–186		18	52	22	22–680	16–22	50	66	60	38	36	70	40	68	48	58	28	30	76	20
(Eastern Standard Time)	Daily	Daily	Daily	Daily	Daily		Daily	Daily	Daily	Daily	Daily	Daily	Daily	Daily	Daily	Daily	Daily	Daily	Daily	Daily	Daily	Daily	Daily	Daily	Daily	Daily	Daily	Daily	Daily	Daily	Daily
	AM	AM	AM	AM	AM	AM	AM	AM	AM	PM	PM	PM	PM	PM	PM	PM	PM	PM	PM	PM	PM	PM	AM	AM	AM	AM	AM	PM	AM	AM	AM
Lv Pittsburgh, Pa.(Pa.Sta.)	2 04	2 35	3 47	7 12	7 48	*8 00	8 23	9 45	11 05	2 00	4 00	5 00	9 00	10 00	10 00	10 25	10 35	10 50	11 00	11 17	11 25	11 35	12 03	12 13	12 23	12 31	1 06	1 28		1 36	1 47
East Liberty, Pa.				7 23		8 12	8 34	9 56	11 17	2 11	c4 11	5 12	10c12	10c12	10c12	10c36	10c46		11c12		11c37										
Wilkinsburg, Pa.						8 16			11 22	e5 15																					
Braddock, Pa.						8 23			11 29																						
East Pittsburgh, Pa.						8 26				5 26																					
Lv Wilmerding, Pa.						8 31			11 36	e5 30																					
Irwin, Pa.						8 43			11 49																						
Jeannette, Pa.						8 52			11 59																						
Greensburg, Pa.			4 30	7 57		9 10	9 06		12 15	2 43	4 45	5 59	10 47	10 47									12 11								
Latrobe, Pa.						9 25	9 18		12 31	2 55	4 58	6 15	11 01	11 01																	
Lv Derry, Pa.						9 33						6 25																			
Torrance, Pa.						9 49						6 42											1 06								
Johnstown, Pa.			5 25	8 52	9 17	10 35	10 00	11 14	12 49	3 37	5 12	7 17	11 48	11 48																	
Cresson, Pa.			6 10		11 19				1 22		5 42	7 17																			
Ar Altoona, Pa.	4 41	5 25	6 42	10 00	10 21	11 50	11 03	12 17	2 42	4 40	6 50	8 35	11 33	12 55	12 55	1 05		1 15	1 30	1 50	1 57	2 15	2 25	2 36	2 50	3 25	3 01	3 45	4 00	n4 16	4 26
Lv Altoona, Pa.	4 45	5 29	6 50	10 04	10 25	12 10	11 07	12 21	2 46	4 44	6 55	8 47	11 43	12 59	12 59	1 09		1 20	1 34	1 54	2 01	2 19	2 29	2 40	2 54	3 29	3 05	3 49	4 04	n4 20	4 30
Tyrone, Pa.						12 37	11 23		3 03		7 11	9 06	12 01																		
Huntingdon, Pa.						1 15	11 50		3 35		7 39	9 33	12 31																		
Mount Union, Pa.						1 30			3 49																						
Lv Lewistown, Pa.			8 05			2 00	12 30	1 35	4 19	5 59	8 20		1 12																		
Mifflin, Pa.						2 23			4 40		8 38																				
Newport, Pa.						3 07			5 16																						
Duncannon, Pa.						3 24			5 35																						
Ar Harrisburg, Pa.	7 05	7 55	9 15	12 24	12 47	3 50	1 42	2 45	6 05	7 07	9 38	11 29	2 28	3 24	3 24	3 40	3 58	4 18	4 23	4 43	4 50	5 15	5 15	5 54	5 25	6 14	6 24	6 55
Lv Harrisburg, Pa.	7 22	8 03		1 50	1 50	5 13	1 50	5 13	7 15	7 15		12 45		3 55	3 55	4 40		4 40		5 25	5 25		5 30			7 22
Ar York, Pa.	8 07	8 49		2 33	2 33	602	2 33	6 02	7 57	7 57		1 30		4 34	5 18			5 18		6 08	6 08		6 18			n8 07	8 07
Baltimore, Md.(Pa.Sta.)	9 45	10 30		4 00	4 00	748	4 10	7 48	9 35	10 30		3 10		6 15	6 49			6 49		7 51	7 51		8 04			n9 45	9 45
Washington, D. C.	10 35	11 25		5 00	5 00	840	5 00	8 40	10 30	11 30		5 15		7 20	7 40			7 40		8 40	8 40		8 55			n1035	10 35
Lv Harrisburg, Pa.	7 17	8 05	9 23	12 29	12 52	420	1 50	2 50	6 20	7 15	9 48	11 59	2 43	3 55	4 15	3 55		4 08	4 45	4 32	5 10	4 55	5 05	5 20	5 59		6 21	6 29	n7 00
Middletown, Pa.						433					10 06																			
Elizabethtown, Pa.						443																								
Mount Joy, Pa.						454																								
Lancaster, Pa.	7 52	8 40	9 58	1 04	1 26	519	2 25	3 24	6 59	7 51	10 28	12 41		4 50								5 55	6 35			7 03
Lv Parkesburg, Pa.						5 47										5 46										
Coatesville, Pa.						5 59	2 55		7 29		11 00	1 12				5 55										
Downingtown, Pa.						6 09										6 09										
Paoli, Pa.	8 39	9 27	10 45	1 51	2 10	6 27	3 15	4 08	7 50	8 37	11 23	1 34				6 12			5 28		5 53	6 40	6 21	6 29	6 45	7 24	y7 40	7 54	n8 23
Ar Philadelphia, Pa. Penna. Sta. (30th St.) Broad Street Station						6 53			8 15							6 39				7 06						
						6 57			8 25							6 43				7 15						
N. Phila. (See page 20)	d9 06	d9 52	d11d13	d2 16	d2 40		d3 42	d4 34		9d01	11 47	d2 19			4 35	d5 42		d5 42		d5 56	d6 42	d6 23		6d49	d6 56	7 10	d7 50		d8 08	8 19	n8 54
Ar Trenton, N. J.	v9 33	10 20		2 43	3 07	7 39		5 01	8 56	9 47	1 06		5 06				6 24			7 49	7w17		7 45	w8 18		w8 47
New Brunswick, N. J.								5 27					5 37	6 30			6 30									
Elizabeth, N. J.													6 00													
Newark, N. J.	v1018	11 09	12d25	3 29	3 56	8 24	4 53	5 55	9 44	10 34	1 52		6 13	6 55			6 55		7 12	d8 02	7 45	8 39	8 07	8 12	8 35	9 05		d9 15	d9 34	n1009
Lv Newark, N. J.	10 21	11 11	12 31	3 34	3 56	8 31	4 53	5 59	9 51	10 41	*2 30		6 13	6 56		6 56		7 14	8 02	7 50	8 44	8 08	8 14	8 39	9 05	9 21	9 41	10 11
Ar JerseyCity,(Ex.PL)(u)	10 38	11 22	12 48	3 51	4(13	8 48	5(10	6 16	10 08	10 58	*2 47		6 30	7(13		7(13		7 31	8 19	8 07	9 01	8 25	8(31	8 55	9(22	9 38	9 58	10 28
NewYork,N.Y.(HudTer)	10 41	11 31	12 51	3 54	4 16	8 51	5(13	6 19	10 11	11 01	*2 50		6 33	7(13		7(13		7 34	8 22	8 10	9 04	8 34	8(34	8 58	9(25	9 41	10 01	10 31
Ar NewYork,N.Y.(Pa.Sta.)	10 35	11 30	12 40	3 45	4 15	8 40	5 15	6 10	10 50	10 50	2 10		6 35	7 20		7 20		7 30	8 20	8 05	8 55	8 30	8 30	8 50	9 30	9 30	9 50	10 30
Lv New York,N.Y.(Pa.Sta.) (N.Y.N.H.& H.R.R.)	11 00	2 00	2 00	5 00	5 00		7 00	7 00	2 30	2 30	2 30		10 00	10 00		10 00		10 00	10 00	10 00	10 00	10 00	10 00	10 00	10 00	10 00	10 00	11 00
Ar Boston, Mass.	3 55	6 55	6 55	10 10	10 10		11 45	11 45	7 45	7 45	7 45		2 55	2 55		2 55		2 55	2 55	2 55	2 55	2 55	2 55	2 55	2 55	2 55	2 55	3 55
	PM	PM	PM	PM	PM	PM	PM	AM	AM	AM	AM	PM	PM	AM	PM	PM	PM	PM	PM	PM	PM	PM	PM	AM	PM	PM	PM	AM

* Daily.

† Daily except Sunday.

(On Sundays arrives a few minutes later.

▼ On Sundays leaves Newark 2.00 A. M., arrives Jersey City 2.17 A. M., Hudson Terminal 2.20 A. M.

c Stops only to receive passengers.

d Stops only to discharge passengers.

e Stops Sundays only.

f Stops only on signal or notice to agent or conductor to receive or discharge passengers.

n Stops only to discharge passengers from Pittsburgh and beyond.

u Hudson & Manhattan R. R. Station.

v Stops only to discharge passengers from points west of Philadelphia.

w Stops only to discharge passengers from points west of Pittsburgh.

y Stops only on notice to conductor to discharge passengers from points west of Pittsburgh.

movement of war supplies, vehicles, weapons and ammunition. The PRR Pittsburgh Division was bursting at the seams and management decided to build a new tower at a new location (MG) rather than rebuild and reopen AG Tower.

ALTOONA ACTION

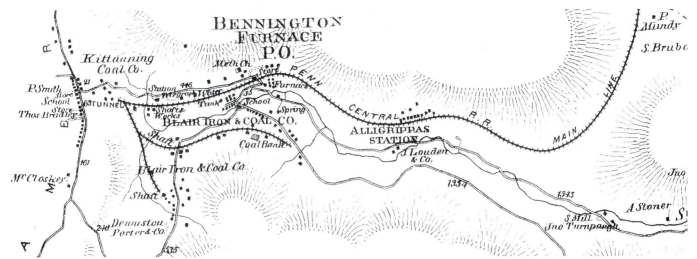

OPPOSITE ABOVE: On March 27, 1977, this is the view from above the four track mainline; a trio of former Pennsylvania Railroad units leads an ore train west of AG. The train is being dragged up the mountain with SD40 #6321, U33C #6556 and SD45 #6204 on the point. The location is just west of signal bridge 2444. Some current sources refer to the whole area between AG and Bennington Curve as The Allegrippus, but the actual town of Allegrippus was about a mile west of here.

OPPOSITE BELOW: After the power has moved along further west, this is the dramatic overview of the heavy westbound iron ore train snaking along the narrow shelf high above Sugar Run. Notice how low the cars are filled, owing to the density of the red ore. The signal bridge in the distance is 2454/5.

ABOVE: Penn Central SD45 #6153 and three more products from General Motors are wrapping their train around Bennington Curve with a westbound freight shortly after the start-up of Conrail in Spring 1976. This train has a pair of helpers on the head end -- note the headlight lit on the third unit. Incredibly, this area was once one of the big industrial centers in Blair County.

MAP: Note how much the Bennington / Allegrippus area has changed since 1873! A thriving coal mining and coke making industry and iron furnace existed in the area just east of the tunnels. Today the area is barren with barely a trace of what once existed here.

BENNINGTON FURNACE

One of the most interesting aspects of railroading is discovering the site of a thriving industrial center at a location that gives few, if any clues, to the rich history of its former importance.

The area around Bennington Curve appears to be the most desolate region of the Pennsylvania Railroad mainline west of Altoona. It is hard to believe that at one time this was one of the most densely populated areas between Altoona and Gallitzin! The buzz centered around a seam of bituminous coal that was found there and the subsequent mining activity, coking operations and iron furnace which appeared thereafter. Finding coal along a major mainline route nearly guaranteed development of a town.

The Blair Iron & Coal Co. owned several mines in the Bennington area and coked the coal in several hundred beehive ovens nearby. Bennington Furnace (for which the "BF" interlocking plant was named) was built in 1846. By the 1880's Bennington Furnace employed 75 people and produced over 13 million pounds of pig iron per year! Pretty amazing for an obscure operation that has all but been forgotten.

Bennington was also populated by workers hired to dig the Summit Tunnel beneath Gallitzin in 1850-51. The work was hard and dangerous and the days were long. Under such conditions it is natural that tensions would rise and tempers would flare. A group of Irish laborers ignited a war among themselves that the PRR could not mediate. Tunnel construction came to a halt as the men feuded. The Hollidaysburg Guards were called in and in three days the workers surrendered, after 33 "prisoners" were taken. It was known as the "Battle of Bennington" and served to quiet the laborers and resume peace in the community. The arduous business of digging the tunnel could now resume.

The town of Bennington boasted nearly 600 residents in its hey-day, including E.R. Baldridge, who was the superintendent of the iron-furnaces, coal- and coke-works... and also the postmaster. It is no wonder that the post office was known as Bennington Furnace.

In addition to the Blair Iron & Coal Co., coal operators known as Denniston, Porter & Co. also had interests in Bennington. This company was organized in 1870 and had become one of the PRR's biggest customers at the time. They employed 140 men by 1880 and moved coal and coke to Gap Furnace (which they owned) and their rolling mills and furnaces at Hollidaysburg, where their headquarters were located.

The Cambria Iron Company of Johnstown also had interests in the area. In 1870 Cambria Iron was the leading producer of rails in the country. The PRR was both a shipper and a customer for Cambria Iron, purchasing rails for their right of way and coal for their locomotive fleet, as well. Cambria Iron bought a substantial interest in the Bennington area and was mining 150,000 tons of coal in a year. As a result, large quantities of coal and coke went west to their works in Johnstown over the PRR. In 1923, Cambria Iron was acquired by Bethlehem Steel.

The fires of the Bennington Furnace were extinguished in the early 1890's, but Bennington's industrial workings lasted well beyond the turn of the century. In fact, mining in the Bennington area took place for over a hundred years. In the 20th century, the Argyle Coal Company began mining the Bennington B Mine. In March 1949, sixty miners refused to leave the Bennington B mine, protesting what they felt were unfair work schedules. After only a few days, the miners emerged, understandably, as the mine was damp, cold, dark and the men hadn't eaten. The Bennington B Mine was closed forever only 5 years later in 1954.

Bennington's location near the eastern portals of the three tunnels made it an important point along the Pennsy mainline. In addition to the carloads of coal, coke and iron that were loaded here, the PRR constructed interlocking plants in the immediate area to facilitate traffic movement east of the tunnels. "SF" interlocking controlled the junction of the New Portage Railroad and the PRR mainline just east of the tunnels. The New Portage Railroad did not carry through traffic from 1858 to 1903, but part of the old grade was used by mining companies to connect their shafts to the mainline. Later, a set of crossovers were placed into service and named "BF". The name was later changed to "Benny".

AUTO-FERRY SERVICE

The Association also recommends that Amtrak investigate an auto-ferry service similar to that presently provided by Auto-Train. The overwhelming demand for Auto-Train service and the fact that Auto-Train stockholders receive a significant return on investment suggests that some type of auto-ferry service operated by Amtrak may prove to be financially rewarding. Admittedly, the Florida route is a lucrative one for Auto-Train service because of the magnitude and nature of automobile travel between these two markets. Whether the same concepts could be profitable on other Amtrak routes is another question, and the answer would require detailed marketing and operating studies.

One area in which the auto-ferry service may be justified in the Region is between Harrisburg, Pa. and a location in the Chicago metropolitan area as shown in Figure 6. A schedule between these two points similar to the current *Broadway Limited* schedule would provide overnight transportation for passengers and their automobiles between strategically located terminals. The major east coast cities of Boston, New York, Philadelphia, Baltimore and Washington would be served through a relatively short drive to Harrisburg, while the Chicago terminal would serve not only that city but also the midwestern cities of St. Louis, Milwaukee and Minneapolis, providing a gateway to the western United States.

For these reasons, USRA recommends that Amtrak perform detailed marketing and operating studies to determine the feasibility of operating an auto-ferry between these two points. The concept of carrying automobiles and their passengers on the same train offers travelers an opportunity to combine the flexibility and convenience of the automobile with the comfort and economics of the train. While Amtrak's service attempts to divert passengers *from* their automobiles, the auto-ferry concept attracts passengers *and* their automobiles. The technology is available now, and it would utilize excess rail capacity.

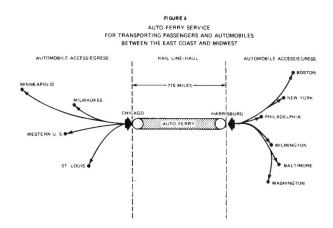

FIGURE 6
AUTO-FERRY SERVICE
FOR TRANSPORTING PASSENGERS AND AUTOMOBILES
BETWEEN THE EAST COAST AND MIDWEST

If such a service does prove successful in attracting sufficient ridership, Amtrak may want to consider providing a second service between Albany, N.Y. and Chicago in order to attract the overflow from the New York and New England area. A further consideration, if demand warrants, could be the extension of auto-ferry service from Chicago to Denver, thereby providing this unique service to Western cities.

Auto-Ferry Service

The Association has used the term auto-ferry to describe a potential passenger service similar to that offered by the Auto-Train Corporation, in which passengers and their automobiles are transported on the same train. Auto-Train's operation between suburban Washington, D.C., and Florida has met with considerable success.

The Plan recommends that Amtrak investigate offering a similar service in the Region, and suggests Chicago to Harrisburg as a potential route. This recommendation appears extremely shallow. Even a cursory review of Auto-Train's route indicates that it is vacation and tourist-oriented, serving the year-round Florida vacation area, terminating in the vicinity of the Walt Disney World amusement park. The Auto-Train rate structure encourages family vacation travel. The major portion of the fare is a basic charge for the automobile and two passengers, with a minimal charge for additional passengers.

Although the concept has been successful, the Office believes its success is dependent on the unique factors of the market it serves. Unfortunately, we do not see any markets in the Region which exhibit features similar to those discussed above.

OPPOSITE ABOVE: Conrail GP40-2 #3297 and B36-7's #5031 and #5015 are westbound on Bennington Curve's track three with an intermodal train in early 1987. In 1947 the eastbound Train #68 "The Red Arrow" from Detroit to New York wrecked on Bennington Curve with a terrible loss of life. Conrail records from 1996 list the curve just east of this location as Padula Curve. Old records indicate that there was a Padula Park and Padula Lake located in nearby Gallitzin early in the 20th century.

OPPOSITE BELOW: At the same location, looking in the other direction, Conrail (ex-EL) SD45-2 #6663 and Conrail United Way (ex-CNJ) SD40 #6285 are approaching the signals at CP-Benny, which marks the east end of "The Slide" for eastbound trains utilizing the steeper line through New Portage Tunnel. The signal 2461E only governs eastbound trains exiting the New Portage Tunnel. Take a good look at the fuel tank on the 6663... you are looking at a tub good for 5,000 gallons of diesel! The SDP45's also had 5,000 gallon fuel tanks, which allowed them to run longer between refuelings, a plus when you need an ever-available fleet of helpers for a busy mountain railroad. This feature undoubtedly was a main factor in the longevity of these units well after the remainder of the SD45 fleet was banished from Conrail's roster.

1156-A16. (Allegheny Division). Overspeed warning system for eastward movements on No. 1 track and no. 2 track between a point 2112 feet west of Mile Post 247 and eastward home signal for Benny, will function as follows:

A--Between a point 2112 feet west of Mile Post 247 and a point 1718 feet east of Mile Post 247, if maximum authorized speed is exceeded the following warning devices will function:
    1. Cab signal will indicate approach.
    2. Eastward home signal at Benny will flash.
    3. Wayside horn at a point 1868 feet east of Mile Post 247, will sound.
    Trains for which warning devices are operated must at once reduce speed to not exceeding maximum authorized speed.

B--Between a point 1718 feet east of Mile Post 247 and a point 2874 feet east of Mile Post 247, if maximum authorized speed is exceeded the following warning devices will function:
    1. Cab signal will indicate approach.
    2. Eastward home signal at Benny will flash.
    3. Wayside horn at a point 3024 feet east of Mile Post 247, will sound.
    Trains for which warning devices are operated must at once reduce speed to not exceeding maximum authorized speed.

C--Between a point 2874 feet east of Mile Post 247 and a point 3674 feet east of Mile Post 247, if maximum authorized speed is exceeded the following warning devices will function:
    1. Cab signal will indicate approach.
    2. Eastward home signal at Benny will flash.
    3. Wayside horn at a point 3824 feet east of Mile Post 247, will sound.
    Trains for which warning devices are operated must at once reduce speed to not exceeding maximum authorized speed.

D--Between a point 3674 feet east of Mile Post 247 and a point 4182 feet east of Mile Post 247, if maximum authorized speed is exceeded the following warning devices will function:
    1. Cab signal will indicate approach.
    2. Eastward home signal at Benny will flash.
    3. Wayside horn at a point 4332 feet east of Mile Post 247, will sound.
    4. Torpedo will be exploded when engine passes eastward home signal at Benny.
    5. Cab signal will flash and cab signal whistle will sound between a point 700 feet east of eastward home signal for Benny and a point 1730 feet east of eastward home signal for Benny.
    Trains exploding torpedo or receiving flashing cab signal and cab signal whistle must be stopped immediately and report to the Operator at AR for instructions.
    Flagman and others will not place torpedoes between a point 900 feet west of eastward home signals for Benny and the westward home signals for Benny.

From the Penn Central Central Region Timetable #1
In effect 4:01A.M., Sunday, April 28, 1968

OPPOSITE ABOVE: Penn Central GP40 #3111 leads another Penn Central EMD and an Erie Lackawanna SD45 westbound under the eastbound absolute signal bridge at Benny on May 22, 1976. Notice the small wooden building for railroad personnel to use on this remote part of the mountain. Later, Conrail removed the crossovers and there is no longer a place for a train to crossover from MG to Gallitzin. This interlocking was originally known as "BF" (Bennington Furnace). From the debris in the foreground, you can tell that it is Spring.

OPPOSITE BELOW: From the hillside visible above the trailers on the previous photo, this is a view of an eastbound symbol freight nearing the bottom of The Slide. Penn Central #6002, an SD35, is exiting Benny interlocking on track one. This view clearly shows the track layout of Benny -- simply put, the crossovers could only be used by eastbound trains moving to a lower track number and westbound trains moving to a higher track number. This view is unique in that it shows signal bridges, a signal mast and dwarf signals all in one scene.

ABOVE: Getting a shove from a Penn Central SD45 and SD35, Conrail caboose #23070 is on a westbound track at Benny. You can see "The Slide" on the fill behind the trailing unit. This cabin is a very early Conrail repaint, photographed on June 26, 1976. It is an example of another N5C in an odd paint scheme, including the name "Conrail" stenciled in gold paint and a gold number. Conrail #23070 is very similar to Penn Central Caboose #23091 shown on page 62.

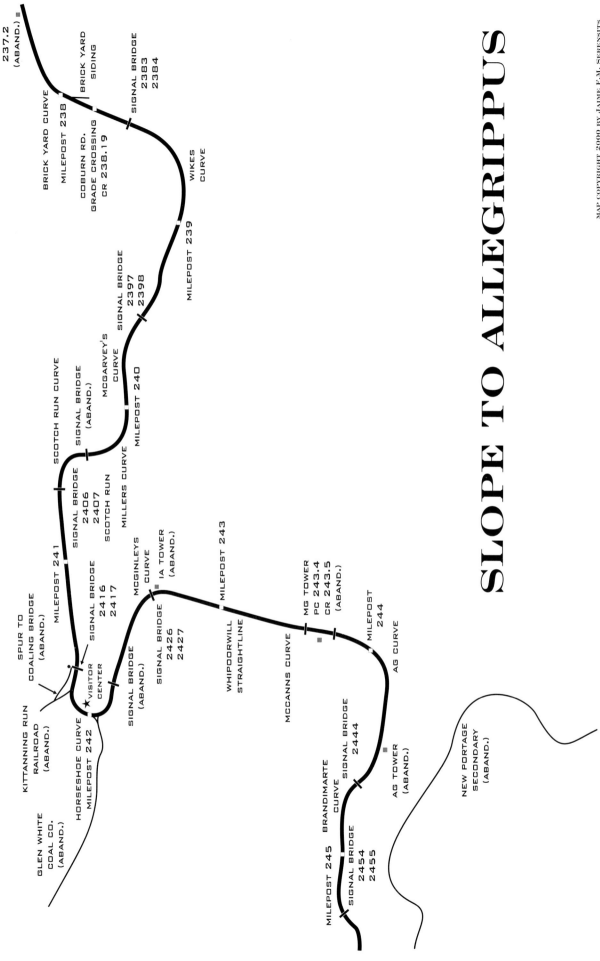

SLOPE TO ALLEGRIPPUS

SLOPE TOWER 237.2 (ABAND.)

BRICK YARD CURVE

MILEPOST 238

COBURN RD. GRADE CROSSING CR 238.19

BRICK YARD SIDING

SIGNAL BRIDGE 2383 2384

WIKES CURVE

MILEPOST 239

SIGNAL BRIDGE 2397 2398

MCGARVEY'S CURVE

MILEPOST 240

SCOTCH RUN CURVE

SIGNAL BRIDGE (ABAND.)

SIGNAL BRIDGE 2406 2407

SCOTCH RUN

MILLERS CURVE

MILEPOST 241

SPUR TO COALING BRIDGE (ABAND.)

SIGNAL BRIDGE 2416 2417

MCGINLEYS CURVE

IA TOWER (ABAND.)

MILEPOST 243

KITTANNING RUN RAILROAD (ABAND.)

VISITOR CENTER

SIGNAL BRIDGE (ABAND.)

SIGNAL BRIDGE 2426 2427

WHIPOORWILL STRAIGHTLINE

MG TOWER PC 243.4 CR 243.5 (ABAND.)

HORSESHOE CURVE MILEPOST 242

GLEN WHITE COAL CO. (ABAND.)

MCCANNS CURVE

MILEPOST 244

AG CURVE

BRANDIMARTE CURVE

SIGNAL BRIDGE 2444

AG TOWER (ABAND.)

NEW PORTAGE SECONDARY (ABAND.)

MILEPOST 245

SIGNAL BRIDGE 2454 2455

MAP COPYRIGHT 2000 BY JAIME F.M. SERENSITS

ALLEGRIPPUS TO CRESSON

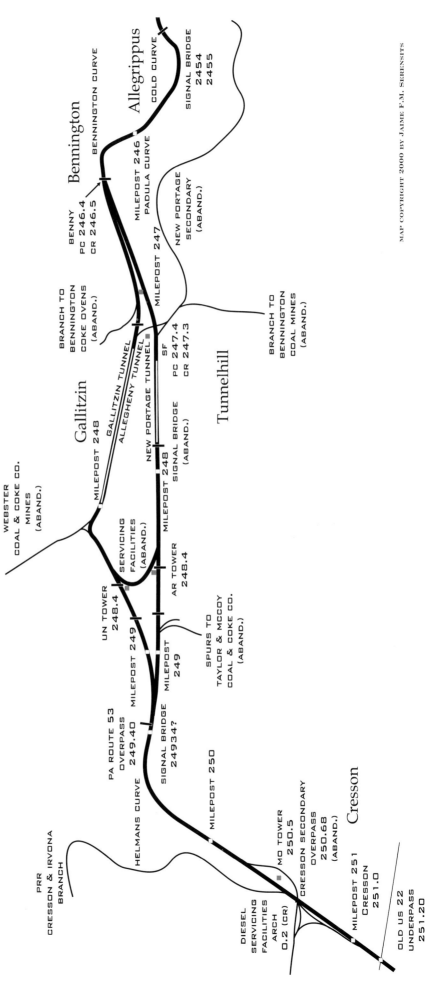

MAP COPYRIGHT 2000 BY JAIME F.M. SERENSITS

Allegrippus

COLD CURVE

SIGNAL BRIDGE
2454
2455

Bennington

BENNINGTON CURVE

BENNY
PC 246.4
CR 246.5

MILEPOST 246
PADULA CURVE

NEW PORTAGE
SECONDARY
(ABAND.)

BRANCH TO
BENNINGTON
COKE OVENS
(ABAND.)

MILEPOST 247

SF
PC 247.4
CR 247.3

BRANCH TO
BENNINGTON
COAL MINES
(ABAND.)

Gallitzin

SPUR TO
WEBSTER
COAL & COKE CO.
MINES
(ABAND.)

MILEPOST 248

GALLITZIN TUNNEL
ALLEGHENY TUNNEL

NEW PORTAGE TUNNEL

MILEPOST 248

SIGNAL BRIDGE
(ABAND.)

Tunnelhill

SERVICING
FACILITIES
(ABAND.)

UN TOWER
248.4

AR TOWER
248.4

MILEPOST 249

PA ROUTE 53
OVERPASS
249.40

HELMANS CURVE

MILEPOST 249

SPURS TO
TAYLOR & MCCOY
COAL & COKE CO.
(ABAND.)

SIGNAL BRIDGE
24934?

MILEPOST 250

PRR
CRESSON & IRVONA
BRANCH

MO TOWER
250.5

CRESSON SECONDARY
OVERPASS
250.68
(ABAND.)

Cresson

MILEPOST 251
CRESSON
251.0

DIESEL
SERVICING
FACILITIES
ARCH
0.2 (CR)

OLD US 22
UNDERPASS
251.20

Dividing and Reuniting. These two views show where the mainlines diverge on the east and west sides of Tunnelhill.

OPPOSITE: It's easy to spot the Erie Lackawanna SD45 in this colorful lashup leaving the New Portage Tunnel on August 20, 1977, and now it's downhill all the way from here to Altoona! Note line on the right -- this leads to the now-abandoned Muleshoe Curve on the New Portage Secondary. The small stone building near the signal bridge once accompanied SF Tower. SF controlled a mainline crossover and the merge of the New Portage Branch and the PRR mainline. This is the point where tracks one and two swing away from tracks three and four to attack the mountain from different angles. At one time, trains routed over the New Portage Secondary could utilize the Gallitzin and Allegheny Tunnels by ducking under the girder bridge carrying tracks one and two overhead at mile 247.21. Beneath the signal bridge you can see the switch off the mainline and the old grade of the branch that served the mines and coke ovens at Bennington Furnace, and there is a remnant of the track left more than twenty years after mining ceased here. Notice all of the ties lying next to track one; Conrail was getting money from the federal government to repair trackage that had been undermaintained for years.

ABOVE: On the other side of the mountain, tracks from the Gallitzin and Allegheny Tunnels swing back to join the tracks from the New Portage Tunnel. In this view, taken from between the Pennsylvania Route 53 bridge and Gallitzin, the rooftops of eastbound boxcars in the foreground are marching toward AR and the New Portage Tunnel. The Penn Central trailer train on track three is a westbound that has emerged from the Allegheny Tunnel and is heading toward Cresson. Track three was known as the westward passenger line because the westbound Gallitzin station faced this track. You can see the wye track in the background, but you cannot see the site of UN Tower, which is located at the junction of the wye and the mainline. It's not surprising to see an ersatz "Conrail" that has been painted on the nose of Penn Central GP35 #2320 by a wag in one of the terminals, as this photo was taken in Spring 1976.

BELOW: A westbound merchandise freight is sneaking through the shadows and is heading for "SF" on the New Portage Secondary, which is an alternate route via Hollidaysburg and Muleshoe Curve. This bypass route between Petersburg and Altoona via Hollidaysburg was physically completed in 1900 when the last section between Aetna Furnace and Petersburg was constructed. It was built to provide an outlet for the limestone that was mined in this region as well as an emergency detour for the mainline. The remainder of the alternate route to the Allegheny Mountain Summit was rebuilt by 1903. For nearly fifty years the New Portage right of way was bare and unused, as the PRR ripped it up in 1858 after purchasing the entire Main Line of Public Works. Much of the rail was reused to complete the westernmost portion of the Pittsburgh, Fort Wayne & Chicago Railroad from Plymouth, Indiana, to Chicago. Plymouth is where the PFW&C met the Cincinnati, Peru & Chicago Railway line from La Porte. In the 1880's, the Terre Haute & Logansport (purchased by PRR in 1898) crossed the PFW&C at Plymouth. Back to the 20th century... Conrail removed one track from the New Portage Secondary in 1955 and the remaining track in 1981, but the new US 22 highway between Altoona and Cresson closely follows part of the route of the old NPS. Notice the "elevated pot signal on a stick".

RAILROADS OF
CENTRAL PENNSYLVANIA

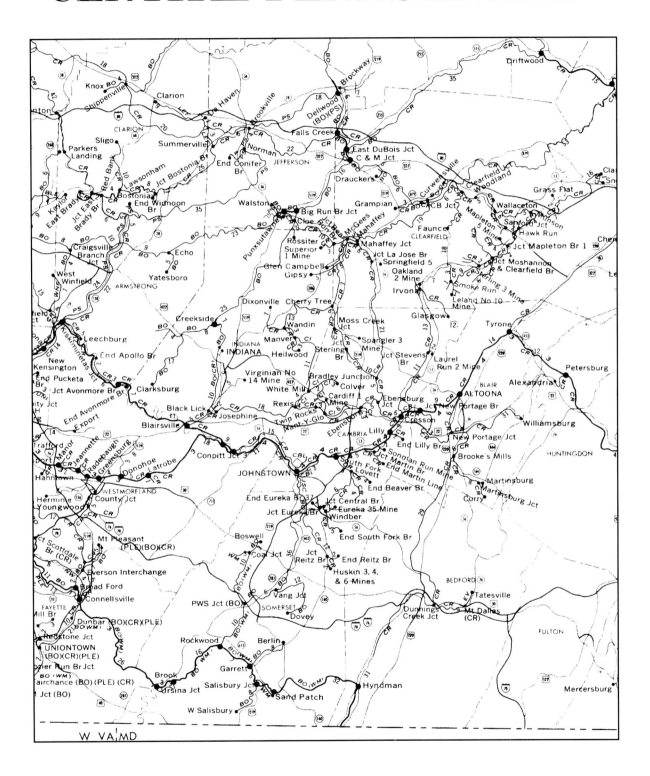

ABOVE: A good overview of the PRR mainline and the Petersburg to Bennington cutoff, plus the railroads and branches surrounding Altoona. This is a Department of Transportation Map published for the state of Pennsylvania in 1976, the year of Conrail's start-up. It was prepared by the U.S. Geological Survey for the Office of Policy and Program Development, Federal Railroad Administration, United States Department of Transportation. The numbers indicate rail miles.

1155-A5. (All Divisions). On March 28, 1966, the Pennsylvania Public Utility Commission adopted in their Railroad Regulations Rule 18 requiring:

"When the horsepower to be used by pusher engine or engines behind a cabin car exceeds 3,500 horsepower, the train crew shall, before such a move is made, vacate the cabin car and occupy the pusher engine or a cabin car behind the pusher engine. The train shall be brought to a stop before the pusher engine or engines are detached.

The practice of cutting off on the fly, pusher engines behind occupied cabin cars shall be limited to those instances in which the horsepower used by the pusher engine does not exceed 3,500 horsepower."

From the Penn Central Central Region Timetable #1
In effect 4:01A.M., Sunday, April 28, 1968

BELOW: Regardless of who owns the tracks, the action on the Allegheny Mountain seemingly never stops, as Penn Central SD40 #6251 and two SD45's exit the now-abandoned Gallitzin Tunnel on track four, while Penn Central GP35 #2354 is heading into Allegheny Tunnel (the original tunnel) on track three. In earlier times, this area was filled with semaphores, tell-tales and such. Photographed in early Fall 1978.

OPPOSITE ABOVE: A pair of Penn Central SD40's are about to shove a westbound freight and its accompanying jade green caboose through the Allegheny Tunnel on May 22, 1976. Signs for mile 247 are barely visible in the distance on this level and the upper level which heads for the New Portage Tunnel. The view is from SF Interlocking, where track two of the New Portage Secondary passes under the mainline approach to the New Portage Tunnel.

OPPOSITE BELOW: In a seldom-seen view from SF Interlocking, three Penn Central SD's running elephant-style lead a westbound piggyback train through the interlocking plant and into the Gallitzin Tunnel at Tunnelhill on May 22, 1976. Note the ventilation blowers bracketing the track three portal. Conrail has since simplified the trackage arrangement here, with no turnouts to contend with all the way to MG. The track heading off to the left is the New Portage Secondary, heading for Hollidaysburg, Altoona and Petersburg.

OPPOSITE ABOVE: Three SD's and a Geep blast from the Gallitzin Tunnel on track 3 in April 1989. The original tunnel on the right (Allegheny Tunnel) was enlarged in 1995 for doublestacks and widened to accommodate two tracks. Today the Gallitzin Tunnel is devoid of trains, and track for that matter, but may one day be pressed into service again if traffic levels warrant. The photo is taken from the Jackson Street bridge.

OPPOSITE BELOW: This eastbound loaded coal train is about to be swallowed up by the Allegheny Tunnel at Gallitzin in 1998. Although many eastbounds use the New Portage Tunnel, an extremely heavy train like this will often use the Allegheny Tunnel to avoid The Slide; the grade on this track is less severe, making train handling easier. Don't let the meager power on the head end fool you, there was a quartet of SD40-2's bringing up the rear! Photo by Jaime F. M. Serensits.

ABOVE: The appeal of PRR mountain railroading is universal, as evidenced by these two visitors from Switzerland photographing an intermodal train being pushed out of the Allegheny Tunnel on June 13, 1998. The town of Gallitzin has embraced "their" railroad and reaches out to railfans and welcomes us readily. Photo by Jaime F. M. Serensits.

OPPOSITE ABOVE: Just like old times! Reminiscent of the days when steam ruled the Alleghenies, Reading T-1 #2102 belches smoke at the entrance to the twin tunnels at Gallitzin on May 15, 1977, while a westbound freight passes on track three with Chicago & North Western, Illinois Central, Frisco and SOO boxes heading back to Chicago. The 2102 was doubleheading with Grand Trunk Western 2-8-2 #4070, assisted by Penn Central SD40 #6321 and SD35 #6017.

OPPOSITE BELOW: Head end helpers consisting of SD40-2's #6366 and #6364 lead SD60 #6849 and another EMD out of the west portal of Gallitzin Tunnel on October 7, 1982. Twelve-thousand-plus horsepower is the rule, not the exception, on the point of trains exiting this tunnel. Notice how the bright fall foliage complements the bright blue paint on these four Conrail diesels... now if Norfolk Southern would only replant the garden that grew between tracks three and four at the the turn of the previous century.

ABOVE: A general look at the reconstruction of the Allegheny Tunnel from the Jackson Street overpass in Gallitzin, taken in early 1995. Notice how the white dust from the pulverized rock is coating all of the equipment. The tracks have been removed from the Allegheny Tunnel in order to complete work on the interior, leaving only one westbound track here and one eastbound track in Tunnelhill. The new bore is capable of hosting doublestacks and is double-tracked. It appears that fresh rock has been exposed above the new portal.

OPPOSITE ABOVE: A wild consist of two Penn Central SD45's, a GP35 and two Lehigh Valley U23B's have just exited the Allegheny Tunnel at Gallitzin and crossed under the Jackson Street bridge with a trailer train on May 16, 1976. Although Cornell Red would have looked good on the point, the LV U23B's couldn't lead because they didn't have the PRR cab signal equipment required in this territory. It appears that the two pedestrians on the bridge were the beneficiary of some heated carbon particulates.

OPPOSITE BELOW: Conrail SD40-2's #6358 and #6368, Ballast Express #6618 and another unit are westbound and have exited the new and improved Allegheny Tunnel. The 6358 has a pair of nearly-purple square plates added around the classification lights, resulting in quite a different look. The photo was taken from approximately where the Gallitzin westbound station was located long ago. At one time, UN Tower was located adjacent to the west side of the bridge on the other side of the tracks. It was later moved farther west to the connection of the wye track from AR Tower. Both the station and UN Tower have been gone for years. The yellow triangle on the signpost is an indicator to the operator of a snowplow to lift the blade at that point to avoid ripping the track lubricator out of the ground. Notice the railroad signal bungalow on the hillside and the 1942 PRR N5C caboose on the far left side of the photo. It is on display in Gallitzin Tunnels Park, along with the new railroad museum and theater across the street. According to the staff, the cost of admission to these attractions is a big happy smile!

MAIN LINE PHILADELPHIA TO PITTSBURGH

Interlocking	Interlocking Station	Block Station and Train Order Office	Block-Limit Station	STATIONS	Distance from Philadelphia	Sidings Assigned Direction. Car Capacity 50 ft. cars		
						West or North	East or South	Both
				PHILADELPHIA (Eastern Region)				
				HARRISBURG	104.6			
X	X	X ★		ROCKVILLE	109.9			
				MARYSVILLE	112.0			
X	X	X ★		BANKS	113.2			
				DIV. POST (Allegheny Div.)	113.4			
X	X	X ★		VIEW	118.9			
X	X	X ★		PORT	133.4			
X	X	X ★		MIFFLIN	153.6			
X				WALL R—Mifflin	157.0			
				LEWISTOWN	165.2			
X	X	X ★		LEWIS	166.4			
				MOUNT UNION	190.4			
X	X	X ★		JACKS	191.4			
				MAPLETON	193.7			
				BRIDGEPORT	196.0			
				HUNTINGDON	202.3			
X	X	X ★		HUNT	202.4			
X				DEER	204.7			
X				PETE } R—Hunt.	209.0			
X				TUNNEL R—Spruce	212.9			
X	X	X ★		SPRUCE	214.1			
X		X ★		FORGE†	220.9			
				TYRONE	222.1			
X				WILSON R—Gray	222.2			
X	X	X ★		GRAY	223.1			
X				BELL	230.0			
X	X	X ★		ANTIS	232.1			
X	X	★		WORKS	235.5			
				ALTOONA	236.1			
X	X	X ★		ALTO	236.3			
X				SLOPE R—Alto	237.2			
X	P	P ★		MG	243.4			
X				BENNY	246.4			
X				SF }	247.4			
				GALLITZIN } R-AR	248.2			
X				UN	248.4			
X	X	X ★		AR*	248.4			
X	X	X ★		MO	250.5			
				CRESSON	251.0			
X				W R—SO	264.1			
X	X	X ★		SO	266.1			
X				AO R—C	271.2			
				CONEMAUGH	272.6			
X	X	X ★		C	273.2			
X				JW R—C	274.5			
				JOHNSTOWN	275.1			
X	X	X ★		SG	277.3			
X	X	X ★		JD	290.6			
				DIV. POST (Pittsburgh Div.)	298.0			

MAIN LINE PHILADELPHIA TO PITTSBURGH

Interlocking	Interlocking Station	Block Station and Train Order Office	Block-Limit Station	STATION	Distance From Philadelphia	Siding Direction: E.W.N.S. or Both & Length in Feet	Note
X	X	X ★		(Eastern Reg.) (Harrisburg Div.) STATE (Cumberland Valley Br.)	104.6		
				HARRISBURG	104.6		
X	X	X ★		HARRIS	104.8		
X	X	X ★		ROCKVILLE	109.9		
				(Main Line Harrisburg - Buffalo) MARYSVILLE	112.0		
X	X	X ★		BANKS	113.2		
				DIVISION POST (Allegheny Div.)	113.3		
X	X	X ★		VIEW	118.9		
X	X	X ★		PORT	133.5		
X	X	X ★		MIFFLIN	153.7		
X				WALL R - Mifflin	157.2		
				LEWISTOWN	165.7		
X	X	X ★		LEWIS	166.7		
				MOUNT UNION	190.3		
X	X	X ★		JACKS	191.3		
				MAPLETON	193.7		
				BRIDGEPORT	196.0		
				HUNTINGDON	202.3		
X	X	X ★		HUNT	202.4		
X				DEER	204.7		
X				PETE (H&P Secondary) } R-Hunt	209.1		
X				TUNNEL R - Spruce	212.9		
X	X	X ★		SPRUCE	214.2		
				TYRONE	221.1		
X				WILSON (Bald Eagle Br.)R-Gray	222.3		
X	X	X ★		GRAY	223.3		
X	X	X ★		ANTIS	232.4		
X				HOMER (Rose Connecting) }R- WORKS	234.0		
				ALTOONA	235.7		
				ALTOONA	236.1		
X	X	X ★		ALTO (H&P Branch)	236.7		
X				SLOPE R - Alto	237.2		
X	P	P ★		MG	243.5		
X				BENNY	246.3		
X				SF (New Portage Sec.) R - AR	247.2		
				GALLITZIN }	248.1		
				UN	248.4		
X	X	X ★		AR *	248.4		
X	X	X ★		MO (Cresson Secondary)	250.5		
				CRESSON	251.0		
X				W (South Fork Sec.)...R - SO	264.6		
X	X	X ★		SO (South Fork Secondary)	266.1		
X				AO R - C	271.2		
				CONEMAUGH	272.6		
X	X	X ★		C	273.2		
X				JW R - C	274.5		
				JOHNSTOWN	275.1		
X	X	X ★		SG	277.4		
				DIVISION POST (Pittsburgh Div)	290.2		

For your comparison we present the mainline timetables from Penn Central Timetable #1 and Conrail Timetable #1.

ABOVE: Two GM products and ALCO Century 425 #2420 are heading toward the New Portage Tunnel with an eastbound piggyback train on January 30, 1972. The power has just passed beneath the highway bridge and the crew can see the top of the mountain ahead of the train. The road that follows along the right side of the train is named, appropriately, Portage Street. The New Portage Tunnel was, and is, used almost exclusively by eastbound trains due to the steep grade.

OPPOSITE: Two Penn Central GP35's and an Erie Lackawanna SDP45 bring a hot merchandise train east through the AR interlocking plant at Tunnel in 1976. There are work equipment and two sets of helper power sitting on the wye tracks and the signal bridge west of UN interlocking is straddling the westbound mainline tracks in the distance. From the time this line was built, the PRR wreck train was stationed here, before moving to Cresson in 1931.

1156-A13. (Allegheny Division). Eastward trains destined beyond Gallitzin:

A cluster of green lights located on the front of AR Tower, when lighted, will indicate to conductor of the train and engineman of the pusher to remain coupled to Altoona. If not lighted they will be governed by the following:

Helpers on the rear will cut off east of the summit, east of home signal bridge at Gallitzin and will be governed by the fixed signal for reverse movements through AR.

A sign reading "Cut OFF Point" is located on the south side of No. 2 track, 400 feet east of Mile Post 248, east of AR.

This sign locates "the summit." Helpers on the rear of eastward trains will cut off east of this sign, to avoid a slack adjustment after the helper is detached.

Westward trains destined beyond Gallitzin:
East Slope helpers on rear will cut off promptly after passing Gallitzin.
East Slope freight helpers pulling ahead will remain coupled to MO, Passenger helpers will cut off at UN.

From the Penn Central Central Region Timetable #1
In effect 4:01A.M., Sunday, April 28, 1968

OPPOSITE: Heading into the New Portage Tunnel at Tunnelhill (the railroad calls it Gallitzin) in late Summer 1978 are EMD's belonging to Penn Central and Erie Lackawanna. This must be a very unnerving sight for crews the first time they see this view from their cab -- it looks like they are about to drop off the edge of a tabletop! Notice the milepost 248 in the distance and the remnants of the double track right of way.

BELOW: A late winter snow is blanketing the hamlet of Tunnelhill in 1970 as "The Duquesne" rolls east behind PRR Tuscan Red E8 #4311 (originally 5897A) and a New York Central "B" unit. You can see a Penn Central freight in the distance waiting for the operator at AR Tower to give him clearance to use the single track New Portage Tunnel after the "varnish" clears. The Main Street bridge no longer supports a position-light signal.

GALLITZIN

Located at the western portals of the "Twin Tunnels", Gallitzin is one of the most famous and popular towns in this area, aside from Altoona. Westbound trains exiting the Allegheny Tunnel are nearing the crest of the grade and provide an exciting display of sound and smoke for onlookers.

In 1877 the fare for the 249 mile ride from Philadelphia to Gallitzin was $7.46. You could leave Philadelphia any day of the week at five minutes to midnight and arrive at Gallitzin's westbound station at 9:48 the next morning -- an average speed of 25 miles an hour, door to door.

On a 1996 Conrail document, just east of milepost 246 is a bend in the track marked with the obscure name "Padula Curve". It seems that in April 1907, Padula Park was officially opened for business on Chestnut Street near St. Thomas. A 1918 postcard reads "Lake Padula, Gallitzin, Pennsylvania."

The New Portage Railroad from Duncansville to Bennington was completed in 1902 and trains began running on the NPR in 1903. The west portal of the New Portage Tunnel actually is located in Tunnelhill, but the railroad considered it part of Gallitzin. Tunnelhill is a very old town whose post office was moved to Gallitzin in June 1856. The NPR actually ran level with Portage Street until 1898, when the a project was begun to dig a deep cut for the railroad. As a result of this, the Main Street bridge was built to carry traffic across the busy mainline. Gallitzin's Westbound Station was located right off of Main St.

Another grade crossing elimination project was proposed in 1905 for Aukenbauer's Crossing on Chestnut Street. In April 1908 an agreement was reached to lower Chestnut Street beneath the PRR westbound mainline near the spur to the coke ovens. The following year the Chestnut Street Subway was opened to traffic. This Subway is still in existence and is used by pedestrians and automobiles.

Almost directly above the Subway a spur headed north to Mitchell's Coke Works. This was a huge operation; more than 3,000 coke ovens were built and many of them still exist today, though their fires were extinguished in February 1953. In 1902, Webster Coal Co. bought out J.L. Mitchell and later that year was consolidated into the Pennsylvania Coal & Coke Co. This area was then known as Mine No. 10. Mine No. 9 was the nearby Cresson Shaft and is covered elsewhere.

The Walter J. Donoughe Lumber Co. was established in 1921. At Chestnut and Donoughe Streets, a lumber warehouse was erected. This lumber company is now known as De Gol Bros. Lumber Co. and is significant because they still get rail service today via some very old and historic track. The spur that serves them is the same one that served the old Mitchell Coke Works and Mine No. 9. The tracks disappear in the lumber yard, but their tell-tale ridges in the blacktop are visible and you can follow them right out of the north end of the facility, across St. Thomas Street and right through several residents' backyards!

Another big coal & coke operation was on the other side of town, south of the eastbound passenger mainline. This operation was known as the Taylor & McCoy Coal Works. David McCoy acquired the rights to mine coal off the land of James McCloskey on August 24, 1881. The Taylor & McCoy Coal & Coke Co. began digging and constructed 240 coke ovens on the site. A branch was built to the New Portage Railroad west of the site of the present AR Tower. In 1936 this mine was closed.

Map of Gallitzin & Tunnelhill

CIRCA 1873

OPPOSITE ABOVE: Helper power consisting of Conrail SD40-2 #6394 and SD40 #6257 passes AR Tower on the rear of an eastbound train on October 14, 1984. Notice the leaves that have collected on the grilles of the two SD's. It is truly Autumn for two of the elements in this scene, as well; AR Tower would be shut down on September 20, 1995, though it is still standing at the base of the Gallitzin wye track. Around the same time, the bay window caboose would disappear, too, along with the majority of the great fleet of blue cabeese.

OPPOSITE BELOW: LMS C40-8W #712 is eastbound at the now-closed AR Tower with a doublestack on the old number two eastward passenger track. Notice that the closest signal bridge no longer has any signals left on it. With the setting sun glistening off the rails, you can easily see the track layout as of late Summer in 1997, including the loop track branching off right in front of AR Tower. The closest switch to you is an uncommon equilateral turnout in which neither of the diverging routes has a straight shot. At one time, a spur with points facing west diverged from the mainline between AR Tower and the curve seen in the distance to serve coal mines and coke ovens belonging to Taylor & McCoy Coal Works south of AR Tower.

1155-A23. (Allegheny Division). Helper engines are to be cut away from train at first stop after passing the following locations:

Eastbound trains
     East portal of tunnels at UN or AR.

Westbound trains
     UN or AR.

From the Penn Central Central Region Timetable #1
In effect 4:01A.M., Sunday, April 28, 1968

ABOVE: Six Conrail engines drag an eastbound loaded train past AR Tower and under the many signal bridges in Tunnelhill on October 14, 1984. At this date, AR would only be around for another decade, while its counterpart UN Tower had been closed and torn down decades ago. The train is about to enter the New Portage Tunnel and head for Altoona. Often a heavy train like this will be sent down the hill through Allegheny Tunnel instead, due to the less severe grade. Evidently the dispatcher felt that this train had sufficient braking power to descend The Slide safely, and evidently he was right.

BELOW: Two new GP30's sandwich a pair of GP35's (2205, 2266, 2288 and 2230) -- and bring a hot 69-car time freight around the big curve east of the PA Route 53 overpass. In less than two miles the power will crest the summit just west of the New Portage Tunnel. The next left-hand curve after the long straightaway will bring the train in sight of AR Tower. This photo was taken by Ken Ardinger on August 21, 1964, and amazingly, all five tracks still exist today!

The rear of this train is passing the old site of Cresson Shaft. This was the No. 9 Mine of the Pennsylvania Coal & Coke Corporation. It was sunk in 1886 by a company called Ashcroft & Powell for the Webster Coal and Coke Company, who, along with Mitchell and Berwind, formed the Pennsylvania Coal & Coke Co. in 1902 and incorporated as the Pennsylvania Coal & Coke Corp. in 1911. By 1915 the Cresson Shaft had reached a depth of over 500 feet. The mine was worked by hand until the 1930's. In 1947 a full-scale mechanization program was implemented and in June 1949 the mine was shut down. The No. 9 is visible on this map of Cresson.

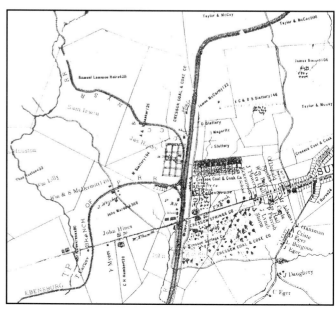

CRESSON SECONDARY TRACK

Interlocking	Interlocking Station	Block Station and Train Order Office	Block-Limit Station	STATIONS	Distance from Cresson	West or North	East or South	Both
				CRESSON SECONDARY TRACK				
				ALLEGHENY DIVISION CRESSON				
		X ★		EP	1.8			
				MUNSTER	3.6			
				EBENSBURG JCT.	6.4			128
			X	KY K-EP	6.4			50
				BRADLEY JUNCTION	11.8			
			X	DF K-EP	11.9			61
				PATTON	18.5			37
			X	PU K-EP	18.6			
				HASTINGS JCT.	26.1			47
			X	RE K-EP	25.9			
				WELSHDALE	30.8			54
			X	LJ K-EP	35.2			
				MAHAFFEY JCT.	39.0			
			X	HM K-EP	40.9			
				McGEES JUNCTION	41.0			
				BEAR RUN JCT.	43.7			
			X	K K-EP	47.8			
				CLOE	54.2			
				PUNXSUTAWNEY	56.5			
			X	RU K-EP	56.6			
				END OF TRACK	63.3			
				BLACK LICK SECONDARY TRACK				
				ALLEGHENY DIVISION CRESSON				
		X ★		EP				
			X	KY K-EP	5.4			
				EBENSBURG JCT.	6.4			
			X	BETH K-EP	10.5			
				EBENSBURG⌒	11.0			55
			X	STEEL K-EP	12.7			
				BEULAH	14.1			72
			X	SR K-EP	17.7			
				NANTYGLO	18.5			74
				TWIN ROCKS	20.5			40
				VINTONDALE	24.0			28
			X	VF K-EP	24.4			
				RITTER	25.0			46
			X	CH K-EP	35.8			50
			X	NI K-EP	42.1			
			X	ZD K-EP	43.3			
				SUSQUEHANNA SECONDARY TRACK				
				ALLEGHENY DIVISION CRESSON				
		X ★		EP				
				BRADLEY JUNCTION	11.8			
			X	DF K-EP	11.9			
				TOD	13.2			
			X	IR K-EP	14.9			
				DISHART	15.0			43
				LUTHER JCT.	18.8			
				STERLING JCT.	20.4			
			X	BN K-EP	21.6			65
				SPANGLER	22.3			
			X	WC K-EP	23.6			
				BARNESBORO	23.7			
			X	JA K-EP	25.6			
				EMIGH RUN JCT. N.Y.C.	27.9			
			X	CJ (CHERRY TREE JCT) K-EP	28.9			
			X	DC (CHERRY TREE) K-EP	29.3			

CRESSON SECONDARY TRACK
(Allegheny Division)

Interlocking	Interlocking Station	Block Station and Train Order Office	Block-Limit Station	STATION	Distance From Cresson	Siding Direction: E.W.N.S. or Both & Length in Feet	Note
				CRESSON			
				ARCH	0.2		
				WATER PLUG	0.5		
				END OF & BEGIN BLOCK	1.9		
				MUNSTER	3.1	5830 B	
				EBENSBURG JUNCTION	6.4	2200 B	
				(Black Lick Secondary)			
			X	KY	6.4		
				BRADLEY JCT.	11.6	3500 B	
				(Susquehanna Sec.)			
			X	DF	11.8		
				PATTON	18.5	1756 B	
			X	PU	18.6		
			X	RE	25.9		
				HASTINGS JCT.	26.1		
				WELSHDALE K-Wye	30.8		
			X	LJ	35.2		
			X	HM (Mahaffey Sec.)	39.1		
				McGEES JCT.	40.9		
				BEAR RUN JCT.	43.8		
			X	K	47.8		
				CLOE	54.3		
				PUNXSUTAWNEY	56.6		
			X △	RU	56.6		
				END OF TRACK	57.5		

Direction from Cresson to End of Track is northward.
△ Indicates in service for southward trains only.

BLACK LICK SECONDARY TRACK
(Allegheny Division)

Interlocking	Interlocking Station	Block Station and Train Order Office	Block-Limit Station	STATION	Distance From Cresson	Siding Direction: E.W.N.S. or Both & Length in Feet	Note
			X △	COAL	5.4		
				EBENSBURG JCT.	6.4		
				(Cresson Secondary)			
			X	BETH	10.5		
				EBENSBURG	11.0	2505 B	
			X	STEEL	12.7		
				BEULAH	14.1	3789 B	
				SR	17.7	3610 B	
				NANTY GLO K-Wye	18.5		
				TWIN ROCKS	19.9	2083 B	
				VINTONDALE	23.9	1100 B	
			X	VF	24.3		
				RITTER	24.7	2341 B	
			X	CH	35.8	2482 B	
			X	NI	42.2		
			X ▲	ZD	43.3		
				DIVISION POST (Pittsburgh Div)	43.3		
				(Blairsville Secondary Track)			

Direction from Coal to ZD is westward.
▲ In service for eastward trains only.
△ In service for westward trains only.

SUSQUEHANNA SECONDARY TRACK
(Allegheny Division)

Interlocking	Interlocking Station	Block Station and Train Order Office	Block-Limit Station	STATION	Distance From Cresson	Siding Direction: E.W.N.S. or Both & Length in Feet	Note
			X	DF (Cresson Sec.)	11.8		
				TOD	13.2		
			X	IR	14.9		
				DISHART	14.9	2090 B	
			X	BN	21.6	3340 B	
				SPANGLER K-Wye	22.3		
			X	WC	23.7		
				BARNESBORO	23.8		
			X	JA	25.6		
			X	DC (Cherry Tree)	29.3		

Direction from Cresson to DC is northward.

Here are the Cresson, Black Lick and Susquehanna Secondary Tracks leaving Cresson as described in Penn Central's and Conrail's first timetables. Conrail treated the line to Irvona as the Irvona Running Track, so stations are not listed in the timetable. The Penn Central's Irvona Branch station listing is on page 113.

OPPOSITE ABOVE: Conrail SD45-2 #6658, SD40-2 #6367 and a trio of GP40-2's have a westbound intermodal train on a roll as they approach the Pennsylvania Route 53 highway overpass near Cresson at mp 249.40. The number plate on this westbound signal bridge reads 2493. The entire train is west of the Allegheny Tunnel and is rolling downhill on track three. It is standard practice to place a pair of helpers on the head end of TV trains, as is the case in this October 7, 1992, photo.

OPPOSITE BELOW: Conrail SD40-2 #6384 and SD45-2 #6662 are helping a westbound mixed freight around Helman's Curve on track four. This is the view from the other side of the Route 53 bridge on the same day. The concrete base marks the location of a former signal bridge that controlled the three southernmost tracks. Once again, Conrail dress blue looks good among the fiery red foliage.

ABOVE: Penn Central E8's #4313 and #4303 (formerly PRR 5713 and 5903) fly through Cresson with a short westbound Train #25 "The Duquesne" early in 1972. Although Amtrak is nearly a year old, there are no signs of the blunt arrow anywhere and this is a pure Penn Central consist from the tip of the pilot to the rear markers. Front Street in Cresson is just beyond the main and MO Tower can be seen far in the background. The black girder bridge spanning the main carries the Cresson Secondary flyover track (mile 250.68) and supports a trio of eastbound signals. Passenger service to Cresson was discontinued in 1960. The Cresson Passenger Station was originally built west of the old Route 22 underpass (then known as the Philadelphia and Pittsburgh Pike) in order to be convenient for patrons of the Mountain House at Cresson Springs, a famous resort of the time. It was later moved to about where the photographer is standing, to better serve the residents of the borough of Cresson.

BELOW: A GP40-2/GP40/GP40-2/SD45 combination is flying through Cresson with a westbound trailer train on March 21, 1982. The signal bridge in the background guards the eastern entrance of the MO interlocking plant on the mainline. The maintenance of way equipment is sitting in the overhead yard located south of MO Tower. Notice the dwarf signal that governs the turnout to the Irvona Secondary, which was originally the Cresson & Clearfield County & New York Short Route Railroad Co., which was reorganized as the Cresson & Irvona Railroad Co. on June 28, 1894, which in turn was merged into the Cambria & Clearfield Railway Co. on June 25, 1903. The C&C was absorbed by the PRR in 1913.

OPPOSITE ABOVE: This is a hotshot freight going away from the photographer and ducking under the Cresson Secondary Flyover Bridge. Look how close the the bottom of the bridge comes to scraping the paint off the roof of 6483. That graphically illustrates why Conrail had to remove this bridge in order to run doublestack trains. In the background, ten locomotives are visible waiting their turn in the helper pocket. Although the overhead bridge is gone, the track heading north still hosts coal trains coming down from Clearfield coal regions. Today R.J. Corman operates this branch as part of their Clearfield Cluster. Coal trains from this region are sent north to meet the Norfolk Southern at Keating, located on the old Philadelphia & Erie mainline, or south to Cresson.

OPPOSITE BELOW: For aesthetic reasons, the going-away photo of this train was placed above the coming photo -- the bridge looked awful cutting the page in half! Here is the view of the same hotshot freight looking the other way as it came toward the photographer as he stood on the north side (railroad east) of the flyover bridge. Conrail SD40-2's #6486 and 6483, SD40 #6315 and GP40-2 #3302 are wheeling a westbound money freight past Cresson's MO Tower on an overcast day in April 1989. The presence of containers and auto parts cars mean that this crew will see green signals for the rest of their trip.

OPPOSITE ABOVE: Conrail GP35 #2301 and GP40 #3206 are on the flyover at Cresson heading from the "north" to the "south" side of the mainline. Most of the traffic crossing this bridge consisted of either empty or loaded coal hoppers. The Cresson Secondary was the link to the Cambria & Indiana Railroad, meeting the C&I at Ebensburg Junction and terminating at Punxsutawney. In Penn Central days, all of the blocks on this line were controlled from the EP (Emerald Park) block station in Cresson. The flyover was removed by Conrail as part of a clearance project for doublestacks.

OPPOSITE BELOW: In the summer of 1976, Penn Central #8096 and another GP38-2 accompany a Reading ALCO on a westbound slop freight. They are passing MO Tower (the original tower was built in 1855, tower pictured is from 1888) and are about to roll beneath the Cresson Secondary. Notice the small signal hiding in the shadows in the lower left, protecting trains coming off the Irvona Running Track. At the time of PRR's demise, this line headed north to a connection with the New York Central at Irvona. PC called it the Irvona Branch and officially it continued to Blandburg (Stroud Junction) for a total length of 40.1 miles. It served the Harbinson Walker #8 near Blandburg. At Conrail's startup it terminated at mile 37.7. Amazingly, Blandburg was once served by the Bell's Gap Railroad out of Bellwood (Bell's Mills) who built a narrow gauge line to Irvona in 1882 and standard gauged it in 1883. It later became part of the Pennsylvania and Northwestern.

ABOVE: Conrail B23-7 #1998 is in charge of an eastbound hopper train which is losing a race to an eastbound intermodal train at Cresson in early 1987. There is also a coal train on the far track which is nearly hidden by the containers and trailers. The view is from the Cresson Secondary flyover. A wye track at the diesel servicing facility is visible on the right side of the photo. At one time there was a turntable and a roundhouse located here. The Administrative Office Building of the PRR, Cresson Division, is the big white building beyond the parking lot. Today it is used by crews and maintenance forces. Front Street is on the left side of the photo and Arch Street follows along the far side of the servicing facility. Photo by Jaime F. M. Serensits.

				IRVONA BRANCH	*		
				ALLEGHENY DIVISION			
				CRESSON...			
				YARD LIMIT	2.0		
				PENNA. NO. 16	9.0		65
				CONDRON..	13.2		
				SANDY RUN..	18.0		
				VAN ORMER..	18.9		
				IRVONA JUNCTION	27.3		
				COALPORT (R. R. St.)	30.2		
				BLANDBURG (Stroud Jct.)	40.1		
				The direction from Cresson to Blandburg is Northward. *Distance from Cresson.			

OPPOSITE ABOVE: Here is an overview of the helper station at Cresson in 1987. An ex-CNJ SD40 and a Conrail bought-new SD40-2 are waiting for their next assignment in the locomotive servicing facility. You can see the Cresson Secondary track on the fill to the right and Park Yard beyond that. Emerald Park (EP) is located at the north end of Park Yard. It was the nerve center for the Cresson, Black Lick and Susquehanna Secondaries during early Penn Central days.

OPPOSITE BELOW: Looking west from the Cresson locomotive facility, an eastbound mixed freight climbs slowly toward the summit at Gallitzin on March 21, 1982. The residents in the houses along Front Street command an excellent view of the daily parade of freights up and down the West Slope. The Commercial Hotel (originally the Callan House), just out of sight behind the train, has been converted into the Station Inn, a bed and breakfast for those of us who do not have a transcontinental mainline running across the street from our residences. Tom Davis, proprietor of the Station Inn, mentioned that the deed for his inn notes that the north side of his property borders the New Portage Railroad. Plans originally called for this line to be built where Front Street is today and some maps show it, but the street was built there and the New Portage Railroad was not built west of Gallitzin. The PRR was originally at "street level", but was later placed on the high fill that exists in Cresson today.

ABOVE: How is this for a nice surprise waiting for you at Cresson in 1973? The 2404 is a rare ex-PRR RS27 (only 27 built by ALCO) and the 7344 (ex-PC 7516) is a stranger to these parts, originally New York Central GP9 #5944. This lashup made up for the abundance of black paint and the lack of sunshine on this winter day in Cresson. On this bright note we end our tour of the mainline railroad action around Altoona. We now present a look back at Altoona at the turn of the 20th century and have included an album of additional photos and an index for your reference.

Reminisence of the City of Altoona, Pa.
60 years ago the years 1885 -87
by an old man in his 80th year

In April 1, 1885 I reported to the General Superintendent, Frank Sheppard (this office is located on the north west corner of 11th Ave. and 12th st. at that time) as an apprectice in the Locomotive Machine Shops and was sent by him to the Master Mechanics Office and assigned to the Erecting Shop No. 1 to Albert Mallory's gang as an assistant with Andrew Vauclain, a brother of Samuel S. Vauclain, who later became head man of the Baldwin Locomotive Co. at Philadelphia for a number of years, Their father, a former official, at this time was on the retired list, but came to the shops several times a week. He with other old retired cronies occupied a large table with individual chairs. Here they sat, read the daily papers, agreed and quarreled and passed their old days pleasantly. Many times I have seen him walking around the shops with his cane teasing the boys and wacking them with his cane.

I will here give a description of the city and railroad shops and persons I knew at that time 60 years ago, very few living now. The city at that time claimed a population of 30,000.

The railroad yards divided the city. The older part of the city is north of the railroads and yards and it is butted up against a very high barren rocky hill known as Gospel Hill. There was only room for three avenues running east and west. Along the railroad yards first was 10th Ave. between 12th and 13th Sts. was the depot. (Note) Avenues run east & west, streets run north and south) and a large Hotel, the Logan House, with a large yard and numerous large trees in the same. An iron fence enclosed it and there was a band stand in the center. The Hotel and yard extended from 10th to 11th Aves. and occupied over half of one block between 12th and 13th sts. The rest of this city block was occupied by Adams' Express Co. Office and on the corner of 13th St. was the railroad ticket office, waiting rooms and baggage rooms. The depot sheds extended from 12th St. to near 13th St. and covered two railroad tracks. The Logan House faced these tracks and shed with a high iron fence and gate in the front of the main entrance to the Hotel. Extending from the main Hotel building towards 12th St. was a Quick Lunch Restaurant conducted by the Hotel and at 12th St. was a stairway to the foot bridge to 9th Ave. over the railroad yards and shop yards with a gate and stairs to the shop yards. This foot-bridge crossed the shop yard between the roundhouse for the Middle Division and both Erecting and Machine Shops and at 9th Ave. and where the Master Mechanics and other shop offices all in the yards. George W. Stratton was the Master Mechanic.

There were only three streets that crossed the railroad yards, 4th St. in what at that time was known as Logan Town. This was a grade crossing across about twenty tracks at the head of the classification yards that extended east to G.D. Office at the end of the yards. The next crossing was at 9th St. at the grade over about ten tracks. The third was at 17th St. over a bridge. The locomotive shop yards extended from 11th St. and in width from 9th Ave. including the railroad yards to 10th Ave. East of 12th St. was the roundhouse for the Middle Div., west of it was No. 1 Erecting Shop, a one story brick building. Next to it running parallel was a two story Machine Shop and next to it running parallel was a one story Erecting Shop #2. These 3 buildings were all connected at both ends with cross buildings with yards between the 3 shops. At 13th St. at the end of the shops was a transfer table. Across from it were three buildings in line with the three other buildings. The first in line with No. 1 Erecting Shop was the Blacksmith Shop. The next parallel was the Wheel and Truck Shop and next parallel was the Boiler Shop and all six buildings were served by the Transfer Table. To the right of the Blacksmith Shop was a round building with a turntable in the center. This was the Tank and Tender Shop. Beyond that was another round building with a tall brick smoke stack in the center. This was the Brass Foundry. Beyond the west end of the Blacksmith Shop was the Iron Foundry and west of these buildings at 17th St. was the roundhouse for the Pittsburg Division. (At 9th Ave. and 12th St. was the Master Mechanics and General shop Office with George W. Stratton M.M. in charge. Close to it was the Boiler House for the Shops.) Between Erecting Shop No. 1 and the railroad yards was a long narrow frame shop used as a Flue Factory. This was destroyed by fire one night. It was not rebuilt. This was in the winter of 1885-86. The General Superintendent's Office was on the north west corner of the 11th Ave. and 12th St. He was Frank Sheppard. The Superintendent of both Erecting Shops was William Ford. His assistants superintendent of No. 2 Erecting Shop was Sam Lloyd. The assistant superintendent of No. 1 Erecting Shop was James Lutz. The Machine Shop Superintendent was Peter Moore. His assistant's name I can not recall. He was a tall man with a very black stragly beard. After serving seven month in Albert Mallory's gang with Andy Vauclain I was transfered to the Machine Shop as an assistant to George Rigg on a plainer. George was a little Englishman and a pleasant man to work with. I liked him. Next to his plainers was James (Fergy) Hawkins. He also operated two plainers. I was next transfered to the Slotter gang on a small Slotter for about three months and then to the second story to the Bolt gang on a lathe turning 500 cylinder head studs and was I tired of that job. The foreman of this department of John Kline. He also had charge of the Bolt Storage room. Here a buddy of mine worked, Stewart Simenton, and a young man by the name of McCormick. I was next transfered across the same floor of the shop to the Brass finishing department. I assisted an old man to file and finish badge plates. These plates were about 8 inches in diameter and the letters on them were, Altoona Shops and the year. They were placed on either side of the smoke box. My next job in this gang was a jobbing lathe, a job I did not like. Howard McCormick was the foreman of this department. Here my services with the P.R.R. terminated in the fall of 1887 at my own resignation. I returned to my own town, Hanover, Pa. and went to work as a machinest with the W.M.R.R. for over five years.

Here was 4th St. extending across the R.R. yards south connecting the north and south parts of the city. There were a few short streets running north in Logan Town from there east you were in the country on a dirt road to the east. At Chestnut Ave. and 7th St. south to the R.R. yards, the car shops and extended east for about a mile. At 7th St. what at that time was known as the Brady Yard began. This was a maintenance of way division at 7th St. and the R.R. was a large brick ice house and numerous other buildings in this yard. Along Chestnut Ave. were a number of storage tracks inside a high board fence. These tracks were filled with old Pullman Coaches that were out of use for a number of years. Close by, along Chestnut Ave. was the Coach Building Shop, a long brick building and next to it along Chestnut Ave. was a building of the same design, the Coach Paint Shop. Close to it was the main gate to all of the shops and the yard. Here also was the Company's Fire House equiped with a large brass steam fire engine pulled by two very large gray horses, also a large two wheeled hose cart pulled by a large gray horse. This outfit was a sight to see coming up the street car track on a dead run when going to a fire in the city. Close to the main gate was the Superintendent's Office and other offices in one building. John P. LeVan, I think had charge of this yard and car shops. In this yard were the freight and passenger car shops, smith shops, a foundry, machine shop, plaining mill and lumber yards etc. All cars at that time were built of wood. From Chestnut Ave., on the east from 7th St. was an Athletic Ground and vegetable garden. Both of these plots were for the use of the Logan House Hotel and from there were residences to the east end of Logan Town. On the hill beyond on the right side of the road were three elevated large water tanks. A small distance beyond was a small stream, a branch of the Juniata River and here was the east end of the Altoona Yards at the G.D. Office.

The car shops and Brush Mountain were about two mi. in the distance with a gap in the mountains at that time called the kettle. Here in 1886 the R.R. constructed a large reservoir on a mountain stream for the use of the R.R. Shops. The water supply at that time and before was a scarce article in dry weather. The city had a street car line before 1885 when constructed I do not know. The line started at 4th St. Logan Town on Chestnut Ave. and ran west to 11th St to 11th Ave. to 17th St. to 8th Ave. east on 8th Ave. to 4th St. but was not connected with the Chestnut Ave. end. About three blocks in the open country on 8th Ave. was the Ball and Circus Grounds. The R.R. yards were on the north side. This carline was operated with small horse cars. When traffic was heavy one way they would hitch more horses to the cars at 4th St., and pull them across the R.R. yard to the other terminal and continue the trip. The passengers would walk across the tracks.

The streets at that time, all but a few, were in bad condition. There were no hard surfaces and in wet weather there was deep mud and they were impassable. It was not curiosity to see a hog in a mud puddle on a main street or to see cows on their way to the foot hills out 9th St. In the summertime these cows of a morning would congregate on the small square at Chestnut Ave. and 9th St. and wait until they were all there, then in single file they would go up 9th St. to the foot-hills to the pasture. In the evening this was reversed. If the street was muddy they took the boardwalk. Very few streets had brick or concrete sidewalks. The majority were made with waste lumber from the Freight Car Shops. These walks were made with long stringers parallel with the street and planks of all kinds and shapes were spiked to them.

Quoted from "A Collection of Local History" recalled by Robert E. Spangler, a resident of Hanover, PA... Thanks!!!

ALTOONA ACTION ALBUM

ABOVE: Penn Central GP38 #7853 and SD45 #6227 break out of the shadow of Canoe Mountain and into the sunlight on May 1, 1972. The two tracks went to three in Penn Central days and today it is two tracks straight through where the old Spruce interlocking once existed.

OPPOSITE ABOVE: With a cloud of brakeshoe smoke, the crack "Pennsylvania Limited" skids to a stop in front of the Altoona Passenger Station in 1967. The baggage carts of mail and express are lined up ready to go, and the crews will work the train with energy and gusto that would make NASCAR pit crews envious.

OPPOSITE BELOW: Forty cylinders and 7200 horsepower are shoving a westbound symbol freight around Horseshoe Curve in 1977. The K-4 is barely visible between the cupola and the Southern boxcar.

OPPOSITE ABOVE: Clinging to the rails for all she's worth, Penn Central SD40 #6255 comes howling down the mountain below Horseshoe in full dynamics in order to hold her train in check. This unit is based in Enola where the track is level and the trains are fast. After changing crews at Altoona, the 6255 will be back to a more familiar track speed.

OPPOSITE BELOW: A couple of SD40-2's in two different Conrail schemes assist a slow freight around the Curve in 1996. The SD40-2's have replaced the venerable Erie Lackawanna SD45-2's and SDP45's in regular helper service. Even the CNJ straight SD40's weren't showing up as often at this stage in Conrail's existence. Photo by Jaime F.M. Serensits.

BELOW: Pennsylvania SD40 #6086 and GP9B #3823 are switching cars near Gray Tower just west of Tyrone in June 1967. This is where the Bald Eagle Branch meets the PRR mainline.

PREVIOUS PAGES: A Pennsylvania Railroad SD40 and SD35 are on their way to answer the call of a westbound train that needs a push up the hill. The sand dunes spread out in the yard behind this set of power is evidence that PRR used these tracks to idle power between runs.

A pair of Penn Central SD40's are returning from another westbound push. Notice that the next switch east is open, allowing them to cross back over to the helper pocket where another set of pushers is waiting. The 6269 is one of forty-five SD40's ordered new by Penn Central. Photo is from the pedestrian bridge at Works Tower in 1972 and you can see the Passenger Car Erecting Shop is gone.

OPPOSITE ABOVE: Two Pennsy SW9's are shuffling boxcars east of Altoona's passenger station in 1969. The 9138 and 9136 were originally 8540 and 8538, but were renumbered for the Penn Central merger.

OPPOSITE BELOW: Unless he is a sourpuss, the crewmembers of most trains on the curve will most certainly exchange waves with the visitors at the Horseshoe Curve park. Photo by Jaime F.M. Serensits.

ABOVE: Pennsylvania E8 #4298 and a New York Central E-Unit are stopped at the footbridge in front of the Altoona Passenger Station for a crew change that will take the train all the way to Harrisburg. This power is likely for a Penn Central TrucTrain, as it has come to a stop on a track not easily accessible to passengers. The building occupying much of the photo is part of the 12th Street Machine Shops.

INDEX

BIBLIOGRAPHY

Africa, J. Simpson, History of Huntingdon & Blair Counties, Pennsylvania, Philadelphia, PA, Louis H. Everts, Press of J.B. Lipincott & Co., 1883.

Albrecht, Harry P., World Famous Horseshoe Curve, Altoona, Pennsylvania Railroad, Altoona, PA, Harry P. Albrecht, 1973.

Alexander, Edwin P., On The Main Line -- The Pennsylvania Railroad in the 19th Century, New York, NY, Clarkson N. Potter, Inc., 1971.

Alexander, Edwin P., The Pennsylvania Railroad A Pictorial History, New York, NY, Edwin P. Alexander, 1968.

Altoona Area Railroad Pictorial History, Altoona, PA, The Altoona Mirror, 1997.

Beeler, Richard E., Altoona's Centennial Booklet, Altoona, PA, Richard E. Beeler, 1949.

Blair County 4-H Leaders, Triennial Atlas & Plat Book Blair County, Pennsylvania, Rockford, IL, Rockford Map Publishers, Inc., 1968.

Bradley, James T., North American Locomotive Production 1968-1989, Irving, TX, Bradley Enterprises, 1989.

Buck, Miss Mercedes, Bicentennial History of Cresson (Cambria County) Pennsylvania 1975-1976, Cresson, PA, Cresson Borough Council, 1975.

Burgess, George H., and Kennedy, Miles C., Centennial History of The Pennsylvania Railroad Company 1846-1946, Philadelphia,PA, The Pennsylvania Railroad Company, 1949.

Centennial Celebration 1873-1973, Gallitzin, PA, 1973.

Clark, Esq, Charles B., The City of Altoona Pennsylvania A.D. 1896, Board of Trade, 1896.

Cupper, Dan, Horseshoe Heritage -- The Story of a Great Railroad Landmark, Halifax, PA, Withers Publishing, 1992.

Espenshade, A. Howry, Pennsylvania Place Names, State College, PA, The Pennsylvania State College.

Gordon, Thomas F., A Gazetteer of the State of Pennsylvania, Philadelphia, PA, T. Belknap, 1832.

Horseshoe Curve -- 125 Years, Mckeesport, PA, Rails Northeast, 1981.

Illustrated Historical Combination Atlas of Cambria County Pennsylvania, Philadelphia, PA, Atlas Publishing Co., 1890.

Jacobs, Timothy, The History of the Pennsylvania Railroad, Greenwich, CT, Bromton Books Corp, 1988.

Klein, Philip S., and Hoogenboom, Ari, A History of Pennsylvania, State College, PA, The Pennsylvania State University, 1980.

Liljestrand, Bob, Alco Reference #1, Hanover, PA, The Railroad Press, 1998.

Lloyd Jr., Gordon, and Marre, Louis A., Conrail Motive Power Review Volume 1, Glendale, CA, Interurban Press, 1992.

Moody's Manual of Investments, Railroad Securities, New York, NY, Moody's Investor Service, various years.

My Pennsylvania -- A Brief History of the Commonwealth's Sixty-seven Counties, Harrisburg, PA, Commonwealth of Pennsylvania, 1946.

Nichols, Beach, Atlas of Blair & Huntingdon Counties, Pennsylvania, Philadelphia, PA, A Pomeroy & Co., 1873.

Paige, John C., A Special History Study Pennsylvania Railroad Shops and Works, Altoona, Pennsylvania, U.S. Department of the Interior, National Park Service, 1989.

Pulling, Sr. Anne Frances, Images of America Around Cresson and the Alleghenies, Dover, NH, Arcadia Publishing, 1997.

Pulling, Sr. Anne Frances, Images of America Northern Cambria, Charleston, SC, Arcadia Publishing, 2000.

Railpace Newsmagazine, Piscataway, NJ, various issues.

Roberts, Charles S., and Schlerf, Gary W., Triumph I -- Altoona to Pitcairn 1846 - 1996, Baltimore, MD, Barnard, Roberts and Co. Inc., 1997.

Schotter, H. W., The Growth and Development of the Pennsylvania Railroad Company, A Review of the Charter and Annual Reports of the Pennsylvania Railroad Company 1846 to 1926 , Inclusive, Philadelphia, PA, The Pennsylvania Railroad Company, 1927.

Spangler, Robert E., A Collection of Local History, Hanover, PA, 1951.

Staufer, Alvin F., Flattley, Martin, and Pennypacker, Bert, Pennsy Power -- Steam Diesel and Electric Locomotives of the Pennsylvania Railroad 1900-1957, Carrollton, OH, Alvin F. Staufer, 1962.

Staufer, Alvin F., and Pennypacker, Bert, Pennsy Power II -- Steam Diesel and Electric Locomotives of the Pennsylvania Railroad, Medina, OH, Staufer Litho Plate Co., 1968.

Students and Teachers of the Department of Social Studies, A History of Blair County, Altoona, PA, Altoona High School, 1938.

Taber III, Thomas T., Railroads of Pennsylvania Encyclopedia and Atlas, Muncy, PA, Thomas T. Taber III, 1987.

The Official Guide of the Railways, New York, NY, National Railway Publication Co., various years.

The Official Railway Equipment Register, New York, NY, National Railway Publication Co., various years.

The Railroad Press Magazine, Hanover, PA, various issues.

The Rand-McNally Official Railway Guide, Chicago, IL, Rand, McNally & Co., various years.

Various documents from the Pennsylvania Railroad, Penn Central and Conrail.

Walker, Mike, Steam Powered Video's Comprehensive Railroad Atlas of North America -- North East U.S.A., Kent, England, Steam Powered Publishing, 1993.

Westing, Fred, Pennsy Steam and Semaphores, Seattle, WA, Superior Publishing Company, 1974.

Withers, Paul K., Conrail Motive Power Review 1986-1991, Halifax, PA, Withers Publishing, 1992.

Yanosey, Robert J., Penn Central Power, Edison, NJ, Morning Sun Books, Inc., 1987.

Yanosey, Robert J., Pennsy Diesel Years Volume 2, Edison, NJ, Morning Sun Books, Inc., 1989.